LOOKING
FOR GARIBALDI

TRAVELS ON THREE CONTINENTS
IN THE FOOTSTEPS OF A HERO

JOHN AND NANCY PETRALIA

ALSO BY JOHN AND NANCY PETRALIA

Not in a Tuscan Villa

Publisher's Note: Looking for Garibaldi describes the authors' travel experiences and reflects their opinions relating to those experiences. Some names and identifying details of individuals mentioned in the book have been changed to protect their privacy.

Cover design: Patti Brassard Jefferson
Cover photo: Patricia Downey
Published in the United States by Chartiers Creek Press, LLC
Copyright © John and Nancy Petralia, 2017. All rights reserved.

ISBN-I0: 0692931511
EAN-13: 9780692931516

To all those who refuse to quit.

...to Suzanne Root who became a lawyer in her sixties so she could help troubled youth in Philadelphia, to Dr. Aaron T. Beck, the father of cognitive behavioral therapy, who in his nineties continues to develop innovative treatments for depression and schizophrenia, to Maria Maccecchini who persists in her efforts to cure dementia, to John Mellencamp who tries to learn something new every day, to Michelangelo who at age eighty-eight created the architectural plans for the Church of Santa Maria degli Angeli, to octogenarian Philip Roth who keeps adding to the world's great books, to Steve Jobs who recognized that his mortality was the reason to live life fully, to Thomas Edison who failed 9000 times to develop a light bulb, to Don Quixote for dreaming the impossible, to George Burns, Leonard Cohen, Florence Nightingale, Muhammad Ali, Jimmy Valvano, Helen Keller, and Jan Donnelly for showing us how to live with purpose, to General Anthony "Nuts" McAuliffe, Admiral William Brown and Giuseppe Garibaldi for never surrendering, to Sitting Bull for being the last Indian to lay down his rifle, and to John McEnroe, Mary Carillo and Brad Gilbert for proving to us that retirement is not the same as finished.

When your time comes to die, be not like those whose hearts are filled with fear of death, so that when their time comes they weep and pray for a little more time to live their lives over again in a different way. Sing your death song, and die like a hero going home.

TECUMSEH

A journey awakens all our old fears of danger and risk. Your life is on the line. You are living by your own resources; you have to find your own way and solve every problem on the road.

PAUL THEROUX

MISSION POSSIBLE

Almost everything—all external expectations, all pride, all fear of embarrassment or failure—these things just fall away in the face of death, leaving only what is truly important. Remembering that you are going to die is the best way I know to avoid the trap of thinking you have something to lose. You are already naked. There is no reason not to follow your heart.

STEVE JOBS

THIS TIME, IT'S DIFFERENT. This time, writing a book is central to the plan. Call it a travel book with a twist: walking in the footsteps of one of the great men of the nineteenth century. I don't know if it's good idea, or if it's a new genre, or if anyone will want to read it. But, it's the book I'm writing. The book we're writing. Nancy and me. Nancy's my wife and co-author. We write together. Alternating chapters. Like our first book.

Last time we limited our travels to Italy. This time, we'll be going to all the places the Hero of Two Worlds lived: France, Italy, Brazil, Argentina, Uruguay, and—Staten Island, too.

Last time, fighting conformity, boredom, drudgery, we decided to live in Italy for one year. Live like locals. Not tourists. Not in a fancy Tuscan villa. By doing so, we mused, we'd become fluent in Italian, make new friends, reconnect with my Italian family, enjoy a one-year continuous adventure. And, we did it. Okay, so maybe I'm not exactly fluent in Italian but I'm getting there.

Last time, the book came later. After we returned home to New Jersey. It was our way of answering all the questions. So, how was it? Were the people friendly? Do they like Americans? What do they think about our politics? Is their government as screwed up as it seems? Did you become fluent in Italian? What was the best thing? The most unforgettable? The biggest obstacle? We heard you had eye surgery in Rome. How was that? Is their National Health System as bad as people say? How are the trains? How about all the immigrants? Will Italy ever be the same? Did you feel safe? You didn't have a car; how did you manage? What did you miss the most? When are you going back? Are you going to write a book?

That's why we wrote *Not in a Tuscan Villa*, which thanks to our publisher, editors, and Nancy's mastery of social media has become a bestseller. Imagine that! Two novice writers producing a bestseller. Believe me, no one is more surprised than I. Even more surprising has been the most frequently asked follow up: When's your next book coming out?

This time, I'm prepared to write. I've read thirteen Giuseppe Garibaldi biographies, accumulated scores of articles, military maps, guidebooks, original engravings, pictures of monuments, and the addresses of the most important Garibaldi memorials on three continents.

Another major change: Instead of one long trip, this time we'll be taking several shorter ones. None longer than eight weeks. Why? I can proffer lots of excuses and partial truths, but the most honest answer has to do with health maintenance. How else to put it? At my age, my various body parts require constant care. It's taken me years to build my current stable of doctors here in Fort Myers, Florida where we now live. I'm not about to change any of them.

Besides. Where else would I find a cardiologist, so young, pretty, and smart, she can make my heart palpitate on demand. And, call me elitist, but I'm impressed that my dermatologist was born in Princeton, went to Harvard, and got his medical degree at Yale. Whereas, my Southeast Conference educated orthopedist can rightfully claim to have repaired body and career of some of the top pro athletes in South Florida. Moreover, since we live in the same downtown condo building, I get to converse with him occasionally on the elevator. It's amazing how much free advice you can get going up or down twenty-six floors. Talk about stream of consciousness, I have a urologist who has the untempered panache to say *go with the flow*. Why would I change him? Nor am I about to amend my routine with my Fort Myers retina specialist who every eight weeks injects my right eye with a dose of Avastin. While I suppose I could find a witch doctor in the Brazilian jungles who could do something similar with a curare-tipped arrow, I'm not about to find out. No, there are some things, like a needle in the eye, where it's best not to experiment. See my point?

Besides. My gait is changing.

My good friend and colleague, Maria Maccecchini, a world class expert on Alzheimer's, once told me about two little known early indicators of dementia: change in gait and constipation. Ever since Maria told me, I've been eating more fruits, veggies and bran to promote regularity. Metamucil, too. It all helps. But, controlling gait is a lot more difficult.

I used to walk without thinking about walking. Now, cognitive monitoring is very much part of the ambulatory process. If I don't think about walking, my right foot tends to drop and drag. To control this tendency, I now consciously walk with my feet a little more spread apart, my steps somewhat shorter. Nothing too overt, mind you. But, tight control. Sort of like driving with one foot on the brake. Or, a toddler taking his first few steps.

I wonder if there may be a side benefit. By consciously controlling my stride, might I be creating new pathways to my brain? Becoming less strident, less aggressive, more accommodating, kinder? Perhaps. Anyway, I like to think so.

Funny thing, when I play tennis, I don't notice the change to my gait. When taking short spurts in short pants, I run fine. Nonetheless, my gait change is worrisome. More so, perhaps, because I sometimes forget names and misuse words. While watching the French Open tennis yesterday on TV, for the life of me, I could not recall the name of one of the commentators. I've followed him for years. I saw him play thirty-five years ago at the Spectrum in Philadelphia. I remember how he stopped the match between points to ask his opponent, the fleet-footed Vijay Amritraj, who had just gotten to a ball way off court, what kind of shoes he was wearing. Vijay loved the question. So did the crowd. This guy was never a top ten player but he's developed into a superstar reporter and commentator, a male version of Mary Carillo. He still writes a column in *Tennis Magazine*. He's been a player, a coach, a promoter, a journalist, an all-around prominent figure in the sport. I can't remember his name.

Recently, while talking with a few buddies I said, I can't ostracize my wife for doing such and such, when I meant to say I can't criticize my wife. That was one I noticed. I wonder how many such malaprops I haven't?

How does it go? After denial comes anger, bargaining, guilt, whatever. For me it's not exactly stages, it's more like the whole bundle. I'm sensing them all. Simultaneously! But, especially, guilt. I feel guilty when I use the wrong word, or if there's a day when I don't work out or don't write. I'm worried I won't get this travel book done before I completely lose my ability to travel.

Did I mention he died at seventy-five? Giuseppe Garibaldi. He died at seventy-five. OK, he had sustained eight bullet wounds over the years. That can't do much to extend your life. I've never been shot; but, damn! I'm about to turn seventy-seven.

Don't get me wrong. I'm physically strong. Strong enough to do at least two hundred pushups every day. Some days I do five hundred. One day, I did nine-hundred-sixty. It's perhaps a subject for another book, but I love the way push-ups make me feel. Pumped. Mentally and physically. As if I could take on Mike Tyson or something. No equipment necessary. Get down on the floor and push. Eight years ago, when I first started, the most I could do was ten at a set. Now, I do forty. At least five sets of forty every day. Push-ups keep me strong. So, carrying bags is not the problem. All the other travel stuff is. Crowded planes. Overbooking. TSA. Red tape. Smaller seats. Narrow aisles. Shit! Narrow aisles make it extra hard to control my gait.

"Where should we start?" Nancy asks.

"Nice," I answer, "or Nizza, as it was called then. Garibaldi was born in Nizza. We can start there. I'd love to find that canal where, at age eight, he saved a woman from drowning."

My gears are in overdrive. So many places to see. In addition to his hometown of Nice, we'll want to visit the three Garibaldi museums: Sardinia, Staten Island, and Montevideo. We'll do Brazil, Argentina, and Uruguay in one trip. We'll save the Italy trip until last. I want to go to Janiculum Hill in Rome where his little rag-tag army beat back a much larger French force. When we get to Sicily, we're going to climb that hill in Calatafimi where he famously said: *Here we make Italy, or die.* We'll go to Palermo where he was treated as a Messiah. From there, we'll cross the Straits of Messina. We'll go to Calabria and Naples. I know, we've been before. But, this time, instead of visiting churches and museums, we're going to follow in Garibaldi's footsteps.

"Let's ask Giuliano and Teresa to help," Nancy says. "They've been wanting to show us around Sardinia. Isn't that where Garibaldi died?"

"Yes. On the isle of Caprera. Remember, it's where Lincoln's ambassador, Henry Sanford, came to recruit Garibaldi for the Union army."

Nancy nods and rolls her eyes. "Yes, I know. Haven't I heard the story a dozen times? Garibaldi wanted the job, but would not take it unless Lincoln agreed to end slavery."

"Yes, yes" I say. "But, remember, if Lincoln had made the war about slavery, the Union would have lost Maryland, Kentucky, Delaware, and Missouri to the Confederacy. Not good."

"Garibaldi was always a little ahead of his time."

"Yup. A year later, Lincoln wrote the Emancipation Proclamation."

Nancy adds, "Maybe if Garibaldi had explained to Lincoln that freed slaves would make good fighters, the war would not have lasted so long."

"Brava," I say. "You've learned your lessons well, Grasshopper. When he was fighting in South America, Garibaldi got some of his best troops by freeing slaves from sugar plantations."

Nancy puts her hands on her hips and looks me in the eye, "But, his best recruit was his wife, Anita."

Nancy's right again. Garibaldi fell hard. *Il colpo di fulmine*, the love bolt. Once it hit him, our hero was toast. He had to have her. I'd love to find that spot. The spot on the Brazilian coast where he first saw Anita. It's just one of the places we'll have to go.

And to Argentina. To the village near Buenos Aires where a sadistic general Millan had him flogged. Gave him that mean scar on his left cheek. From Buenos Aires, it's just a hop skip to Montevideo where the Red Shirts were formed, where his family lived during that terrible siege, where he became a Uruguayan national hero, and where his daughter, little Rosa, perished. His Montevideo house is now a museum. We have to go there. I want to stand in the very spot where the great Admiral William Brown stood when he came to pay his respects to his most elusive adversary.

Don't get me wrong. Writing a book is not easy. It takes a lot of discipline, concentration, and hard work. What is it JFK said about going to the moon? We go because it's hard. Or, am I thinking about what it says on my T-shirt? *Just do it.*

"Honey," I say, "I don't care if we have to go to the moon to find him. He's out there. Giuseppe Garibaldi. Unifier of Italy, Admiral, General, Gaucho, Statesman, Hero of Two Worlds. He's out there. Not the statue in the piazza. Not the cartoon character painted by Alexander Dumas and those other ass-kissers. I want to know the real guy. The forgotten hero. His essence. We're gonna find him and write about him."

Nancy smiles. "I didn't know he was lost."

"Okay. Okay. I know. I'm starting to sound like a religious zealot. But, I did promise our fans a different kind of travel book. Let's do what we promised."

Nancy looks at me as if I've asked for a divorce, and says, "*We* promised?"

"Okay. Okay. *I* promised. What's the difference? Anyway, we're not doing it just for our fans. We're doing it for ourselves, too. We're doing it because it's hard. We're doing it because organizing a zillion disparate observations into a coherent story is hard. Like doing nine-hundred-sixty pushups in a day is hard. Like controlling my gait is hard. Shit! We're doing it for anyone who appreciates the effort that goes into crafting a good story. Like that tennis commentator. Not John McEnroe. The other guy. The bald guy. The guy that always cracks me up. What's his name?"

Nancy laughs. "Oh, you mean—"

"Brad Gilbert," I shout. "How could I forget his name? Yes, yes. Brad Gilbert. Let's do it for Brad."

Nancy looks at me with one of her looks, and says "You want to dedicate a book about Giuseppe Garibaldi to a tennis commentator? Well, if nothing else, it'll be different."

Playing Sancho Panza

Every autobiography is concerned with two characters, a Don Quixote, the Ego, and a Sancho Panza, the Self.

W.H. Auden

ANOTHER BOOK. He wants to write another book.

"It'll be fun," he says. "We'll do it together. Like the last time."

That year we spent in Italy—we always say it was the best year of our lives. Adrift in another culture, cut loose from our normal responsibilities with time to do just as we pleased—that's what I loved. It was never intended for a book. When we got home, though, and found ourselves answering the same queries over and over, that's when we thought about one. Writing it wasn't fun—not for me. It was hard work. I admit, after I got into it, when I figured out what I wanted to say about the differences between our two cultures, it got better. In many ways it brought back all the feelings I had about the year, about Italy. I even cried over it several times. But fun? No, it wasn't.

Now he wants to do it again. *Easy for him to say.* I tell people I'm the narrator and he's the commentator. As the narrator, I have to conjure up all the details. The commentator gets to reflect on our situation, tell a pithy story, make the reader laugh with a punchline. Don't get me wrong, being pithy is hard work, but it's not whacking your way through a jungle of details to draw the picture for the reader. My days filled with searches for names of tiny museums or restaurants or the exact name of a festival. Where was that house with the cascade of bougainvillea? What time of year was our visit to Deruta? Did the bus actually take us past that church? How do you say that in Italian? You've got to get it right, because readers know the difference. Thank God for the journal I kept, and thousands of photographs. I got bleary-eyed reconstituting our travels from skimpy notes and squinting at hundreds of pictures. Writing, revising, then writing again. He seems to relish it—the mental gymnastics of crafting a story from disparate parts, juxtaposing time and place. I'm exhausted by the where, the what, the *now*. Then, after it's edited and re-read seven or eight times by different people— some of them in Italy—we get one-line Amazon reader reviews like, "Don't expect to learn Italian from it." *No kidding.* And, "They misspelled many Italian words." Makes you want to guzzle some grappa.

When it was finished, and published, I was glad for the chance to get back to the things I'd put off since before we went away. Days spent in the clay studio with my ceramic sculpture. Books piled around in the house calling "read me." Then, just after the publication date, our house finally went under agreement. On the market for two summer seasons, we'd just about given up hope until the next one when the deal came in. It was late September. The buyers wanted to settle in the spring which was fine with us. We'd have plenty of time to decide where to go. Back to Italy? Another continent? An RV around the USA? Or something else.

Over dinner the evening we signed the papers John joked, "We just have to hope there's not a hurricane." I laughed with him and we toasted our good fortune.

Then Superstorm Sandy hit.

We evacuated with a few clothes, the computers, and some family items. Two days later we were told we couldn't go back for six months. Six *months!* With gas lines cut, and four feet of sand in the only road, it didn't look good. Ultimately it wasn't that long. We had virtually no damage and our sale went through. But in the meantime we went looking for a new place to live. Someplace *not* on a barrier island. Settling into an aerie apartment overlooking the mile-wide

Calusahachee River in Fort Myers— eight miles from the Gulf—*that* was fun. I put off more reading and finding a ceramics studio while I scoured consignment shops and pondered paint colors. We unpacked the few things we'd brought and our books, quite a number about Giuseppe Garibaldi, John's latest passion.

"You know, he lived on three continents," my husband argues. "We can visit them all."

"The travel's appealing. We've talked about going to Argentina for a long time. That would be nice." John's father grew up in Argentina so I've always thought we should see it. I understand Buenos Aires is a beautiful city—very European. A chunk of time there would be fabulous. Sort of like our Italy trip, but not so long. It's Spanish, not Italian. But I'm sure we'll figure out how to get by. And, it's where tango originated. I'm just not sure about the writing.

John keeps working on me, telling me about Garibaldi's exploits and the amazing things he did. I admit, he's growing on me. A guy I can admire. A hero. With flowing blonde hair and casual, sort of cowboy attire, he wasn't just brave, he was dashing. Following him around might be interesting. What might we discover—about Garibaldi, about the world, about ourselves?

One day John says this trip's not going to be visiting churches and museums, but the locations Garibaldi fought and lived. Now wait a minute! If he thinks we're going to Buenos Aires and not seeing the museums and Evita's grave, he's not going with *me*. "I don't want to write a history book," I tell him. "You're the one fascinated with Garibaldi. *You* write the book."

"No, no," he says. "Not a history. John and Nancy traveling, enjoying the experience. On the Garibaldi trail. I'll worry about the Garibaldi stuff. You do the scenery."

Right, the scenery, the part that makes readers believe they're with us. The hard part. A few days later I ask him, "Can we go to Puglia? We said the next time we went to Italy we'd go to Puglia. I want to see the *trulli* houses."

"Sure, sure. Garibaldi was in the south, so, yes, we can go to Puglia."

So, Argentina and Puglia. Two on our list. That part I like.

We've already started to get sucked into life here in Southwest Florida. Trying to figure out our new community, we signed up for theater, opera, symphony and several organizations. The calendar is overcrowded. As the "season" plays out we're constantly weary from doing too much. We bought this place so we could close the door and leave. Now we've tied ourselves tight to *here*. The escape of travel beckons. Once we strip away the "commitments" we've created, it'll be just the two of us again. No longer cinched to a calendar. Back to the shared adventure. Exploring, messing up, figuring it out, discovering the unexpected. Back to leaning on each other. Pooling our strengths.

Living in the actual moment. That feels so much better than negotiating which Friday night event to attend. *I want that feeling back.* That feeling of floating free, open to serendipity, with the freedom to plop down for a couple hours to relax in a cafe or a park. No schedule. The unspoken focus is us—together. His hand cradling mine. Connected, our eyes telegraphing before a word is spoken. Our normal life vanishes. There is no schedule, no phone calls, no meetings, no musts. There's only the wonder of discovery, and yes, the stumbling—both cultural and literal—that crystalizes our commitment to the now. To each other. It's only when we slip the bonds of home that we can pull it off. Hard as it is, I'd travel forever to live like that.

Sometimes now we operate in parallel worlds, checking in a few times each day, but not really together. It's not like we've drifted apart as much as we've turned our focus outward. If we go, there will be just one world—the one we're in together—and I hope we'll rediscover the connectedness we had in Italy.

For that, I'll agree to write.

LOOKING FOR A HERO

When I was a boy, I always saw myself as a hero in comic books and in movies. I grew up believing this dream.

ELVIS PRESLEY

NICE, FRANCE

Don't call us tourists. At least, not typical ones. We're here in Nice not because it's on the Riviera but because this is where Giuseppe Garibaldi was born on July 4, 1807. That's right. Born on America's Independence Day. No wonder the great freedom fighter always had a soft spot in his heart for the Red, White and Blue.

Back in 1807, Nice was part of the Kingdom of Piedmont-Sardinia and was called by its Italian name, Nizza. But, in 1859, in a complex peace agreement among Austria, France and Piedmont-Sardinia, the port city reverted to French rule.

For all his internationalism, Garibaldi never lost his connection to his hometown. Whether he was in South America, Italy, or on the China Seas, to him Nice was never French. Nizza was Nizza. Nizza was where his parents lived, where he grew up speaking Italian, where he brought his family after fourteen years in South America, where, even as a child, his heroics distinguished him as a local hero.

After his death in 1882, the town fathers renamed a square previously named for a Sardinian King to Place Garibaldi. In the middle of the square, you'll find a beautifully crafted fountain featuring a huge bronze statue of our rugged hero standing boldly facing Italy.

Today, Place Garibaldi, with its ochre painted buildings and Piedmontese inspired restaurants, couldn't be more Italian. A few hours ago, at Grand Café de Turin located a stone's throw from the fountain, Nancy and I enjoyed a superb Italian dinner featuring grilled sardines wrapped in lemon leaves. Our one concession to France: A 2010 Sancere. Per usual, I drank three-quarters.

Right now, I'm walking alone along a poorly lit canal where the air smells brackish and the African wind insists on coaxing scores of loosely-rigged halyards to beat out rhythms ill-suited to my controlled gait—and my purpose. It's 1:00 a.m. I can't sleep. Too much wine. Nancy's safely tucked in bed a few blocks back at the Le Meridien hotel. And, I'm on a mission: Find the spot where Garibaldi jumped into the canal.

According to his biographer, Peter de Pollnay, our hero, at age eight, saved the life of a woman who had fallen into a canal. This canal. Quay Papacino. His home base. He dove right in after her. The eight-year-old rescued a drowning woman. Pulled her out. Garibaldi's reward: a severe cold and fever that nearly killed him.

Believable? I don't know. In Dennis Mack Smith's telling, the incident occurred outside of town by a stream, not here on the quay. But, I'm here now, so why not look. Perhaps, there's a commemorative plaque. Anyway, for purely literary reasons, I prefer the de Pollnay version. Why? Because de Pollnay's version is tied to a more gripping story about a thirteen-year-old Giuseppe, Beppe for short, and his then girlfriend Giuseppina, Beppa for short.

As the story goes, Beppa's father was a political refugee from Spain, a worldly man who helped expose young Beppe to exciting new books and revolutionary ideas. The teens saw each other almost daily. One summer day, Beppa and her father went out in a small boat to get mussels off the rocks. The sea was calm, the sun shone; nothing could make one suspect a violent storm was brewing. When it did, waves smashed the frail boat against a jetty. From the shore, Garibaldi could see Beppa and her father holding on to what was left of the smashed boat. He swam out to help. "Save my father, I'll be fine," the brave girl cried. Beppe listened to Beppa; he pulled the father to the beach. But, by the time he returned for Beppa, the sea had taken her.

In years to come, de Pollnay tells us, Garibaldi would rescue many others from drowning. But, he would never forgive himself for Beppa's drowning. And, while he would often return to Nizza to visit his parents and Beppa's family, he never did revisit the spot on the beach where young love died.

As a writer now myself, I'm always looking for ways to organize unrelated ideas into meaningful themes. So, I have to admit I find de Pollnay's tales of Garibaldi's childhood a useful metaphor for my own exploration of the Garibaldi legend. For me, Beppa's story epitomizes a theme that repeats throughout Garibaldi's life: Heroics followed by tragedy: Proof that the world is unfair. The realization comes to us all eventually. But when you're young, at least when you're young in 1950s America, like I was, you think that justice will always prevail—like on the radio where the Lone Ranger, Superman and The Shadow always balance the scales. Now in my seventies, as I dodge logs of dog shit along the dark quay, I can't help wondering how I could have been so young, so naive.

September, 1953. I was on my bike delivering The *Philadelphia Evening Bulletin* on South Bouvier Street between McKean and Mifflin when I looked up to see a baby carriage rolling slowly backwards down the sidewalk from McKean. I quickly pedaled up to the carriage, stuck out my arm, grabbed the handle, looked inside, saw a sleeping baby; I jumped off my bike and let it and my bag full of papers fall to the sidewalk; then, I slowly walked the carriage back to where it must have originated: Claire's Baby Store. After locking the wheels. I poked my head inside the store where I saw two women conversing. My announcement: "I just stopped your baby from rolling down the street" brought both women quickly outside. One, the mother, seeing the carriage parked and locked securely in its place screamed, "Don't you DARE scare me like that!" She then picked up the baby, turned on her heels and went back into Claire's Store. Claire—the other woman—looked at me, shrugged her shoulders, said thank you, followed her customer back into the store and closed the door behind her.

Thank you! That's all I get? Thank you! For saving a baby's life? Thank you. That's it?

I continued on my route.

My route. I had cobbled it together over several months by trading outlying patrons with several other carriers so that my restructured route was concentrated over a tight four square block area around where I lived on South 18th Street. I knew all sixty-one of my customers by their last names. And, they knew me. To them I was Johnny the paperboy or as they pronounced it in South Philly, Johnny the pay-pa-boy. Among my delivery points was a four-story apartment building with the prosaic name of the Fulton Manor. Located at the southwest corner of 17th and McKean, its white sandstone façade with the six-foot-wide chiseled plaque 'Fulton Manor' stood in stark contrast to the encroaching rows of brownstone and brick that surrounded it.

Depending on the day of the week, the Manor could be either the last or first stop on my route. Ensconced inside were eleven customers. Not only did the building represent a welcome sanctuary from the weather, it was also where I got to deliver papers to apartment 104. That's where Jackie T, roughly my age, thirteen, lived with her mother, Mrs. T. If there was a Mr. T, I never saw him. Both Jackie and her mom had looks and style that would catch anyone's eye. In her well-pressed skirt and blouse, and sensible heels, Mrs. T could have been a secretary, maybe a librarian. Too pretty for a teacher. Certainly, none of the nuns who taught us at Saint Monica's looked anything like Mrs. T. But I remember how she could turn even this bumbling teenager into a prominent citizen simply by announcing, as she opened her apartment door, Johnny the newspaper boy. So, nice to see you. Not just any old pay-pa-boy, mind you. Not, simply, Johnny. She bestowed my full title: Johnny the newspaper boy. Each syllable pronounced. Straight stance. Not a hair out of place. White teeth. Pretty smile. Full red lips. Gorgeous figure. Every Saturday, a twenty-five cent tip.

When delivering to 104, I made sure it was done with a thud. Unfortunately, most times, the response I got came not from 104, but from 105 where an old witch wearing the very same powder blue chenille bath robe she wore yesterday, last week, everyday would repeat the same routine: *Thud.* Her door opens just wide enough to flash her crusty robe; satisfied yet again that I am the same annoying pay-pa-boy from yesterday, she quickly slams the door. *Bang.* On those few lucky occasions when my broadcast actually produces Jackie or Jackie's mom, the witch stays clear.

Apartment 104. I don't know whom I yearned for more, Jackie or her mom. Maybe a three-some? Did I even know what that meant back then? Not sure. But, they liked me; they really liked me. At least they acted that way. Twenty-five cent tip, every Saturday.

On this particular Monday, at about 4:00 p.m. My deliberate thud produced the desired effect: Jackie standing in the doorway, smiling.

"Hi, Johnny. How are you?"

Wearing blue jeans, pressed white shirt, no socks, white low-top Keds, blond hair, pixie cut, like her mom's, like Jean Seberg the actress. No make-up. Cute. Very slim. A little too slim, perhaps. Small boobs, unlike her mom. I wonder if she'll invite me in? I wonder if mom's home?

"H-H-H-Hi, Jackie. Good. How's school?"

Stupid thing to say. How's school? Why do I lose my tongue—my brain—in these situations? I wish I had a sister to teach me the ropes. Three brothers. No help. I go to an all boys' school. My mom and dad are from Sicily. Old school. No help. I could use some coaching. Should have asked her if she wants to meet me later for a Coke. Or, said something about music, something cool. Instead I ask How's school? How dumb is that? Stupid. Stupid. Stupid. Shit, Shit. Shit. Stupid shit.

"Oh, Okay, Johnny. Lots of homework. Can't wait 'til Friday night. There's a dance at Southern. My mom is teaching me all these great steps. I love dancing. What about you? Have you been to Neumann's Saturday dances? They're great."

"Uh, no. I haven't been—yet."

Shit, Shit, Shit. That was stupid. I missed an opportunity there. She even goes to our dances. I could have just told her I'd see her there. It wouldn't be like asking her for a date. I could just see her there. Ask her to dance. Instead I act like a geek. Stupid. Stupid geek. Dumb stupid geek. Shit. Shit. Shit.

While my brain squeezes itself deeper into a smaller and smaller black hole, my hands do not know where to go. My white canvas Bulletin bag is off my shoulder. No help there. I could pick it up but that would signal I'm ready to go. Don't want that. My right hand finds the wall. It's looking for something to fiddle. Ah, here's something. This round red glass thing with a little hammer attached by a chain. Looks inviting. I'm touching it. Barely touching it, mind you. See, the glass is not broken. Not a scratch. The little hammer remains in its little holster.

The blue-robed witch is screaming Fire! Fire! Fire! An elderly man using a walker stumbles out of 106. I hear footsteps and screams coming down the steps. The alarm won't quit. I grab my canvas *Evening Bulletin* bag, shout "Shit," put my head down, run out the front door, wrap the canvas bag to my Schwinn's handle bars, and pedal as hard as I can south on 17th Street to Snyder, right on Snyder to 18th, north on 18th to 2034, home. Safe.

Setting off a false fire alarm is a serious offense. At my school, Bishop Neumann High, firemen had come to lecture us boys—Neumann was all boys—about the dangers of false alarms. Firemen had been seriously injured, even killed rushing to false alarms. Setting a false alarm could get the perpetrator dismissed from school, or worse, jail time. I was in trouble. Seriously deep shit.

I told my mother I was tired from a hard day of school and paper deliveries. I expected an argument, but instead she gave me some "little soup"—no matter the type of soup my mother served, when it was for her boys, it was always "little soup." I give you 'little soup, you go to bed.' In bed, I hid deep inside the covers, and waited for the police, the fire department, maybe even the FBI, I don't know. They did not come. The police never came. No one came. Whew.

The next day was Tuesday, fat paper day, the day all the stores ran their full page ads in time for Wednesday, the big shopping day in Philadelphia. The major department stores, Wanamaker's, Strawbridge & Clothier, Lit Brothers and Gimbels, all ran massive ads. On Tuesdays, papers were so fat, I could not deliver on my bike because sixty-one gigantic papers in my canvas carrier made the bike too unbalanced. On Tuesdays, I always carried my canvas bag with sixty-one papers on my shoulder. I tried to get one of the other carriers to deliver my eleven papers to the Fulton Manor. No takers. There was no way around it, I had to go back in there, but only at the end of my route, only after I had delivered the other fifty papers would I go back to the Fulton Manor.

They call them sneakers because they really are sneaky. I am more cat than paper boy.

Not a sound, as I creep down the hall to place the Tuesday Bulletin at 104. Easy does it. No thud. Quiet.

"Johnny, I need to speak with you." It's Mrs. T.

Shit, now I'm in for it. She's pissed at me. Maybe I should tell her about the baby I saved yesterday. How about that, Mrs. T? Doesn't that count? That baby could have been crushed under the wheels of a car. Or, kidnapped, even. I saved a baby's life and all you want to talk about is the stupid fire alarm.

"What happened yesterday, Johnny? Did you do something to the alarm? Do you know you scared the entire building? There were police and firemen. Angry firemen. All these old folks. Very frightening for them, too. What happened? What did you do? Explain!"

I did not have to turn around to know the two laser beams cutting deep into the back of my head were coming from 105.

"Mrs. T. It just went off. I swear. Ask Jackie. I was talking to Jackie. I did not purposely set off the alarm. Honest. My hand just brushed the glass. Brushed it, really. Just a slight touch, like this—"

I am not sure how it was possible, but Tuesday's alarm screamed ten times louder than Monday's. Like Monday, I did not hesitate. I turned, put my head down, made my escape carrying my white canvas *Bulletin* bag with ten undelivered papers.

Again, the police never came.

Perhaps, it's my scarred macula, or maybe it's the wine, or both, but the moonlight off the water now looks like Picasso on LSD. Images flash through my mind. Cut up pictures reassembled in my brain. What if the police had found me, arrested me, jailed me? How different might my life have been?

Jails. They never fazed Garibaldi. He'd either escape or get released because, well because, he was Garibaldi. In 1834, after a failed coup in Genoa, he escaped to here, to Nizza, where he was captured and locked up in a make-shift cell. An hour later he was gone. Escaped through a window fifteen feet off the floor. Dove into this canal. Made it to a boat headed for Marseille and then to Rio de Janeiro.

Time to head back to Le Meridien. Nancy will be worried.

With only my iPhone for light, my fumbling around awakens my sleepy wife. "Are you OK? Where have you been? What time is it? You really had me worried."

"Oh, I couldn't sleep; took a short walk. Thinking. Getting my thoughts organized. About Garibaldi. You know, some of those stories we thought were concocted fairy tales? Well, I'm beginning to think they might be true."

Nancy squints a smile and replies "That's nice, Honey. Now, come to bed."

"You know, he came back to Nice many times in his life but he could never return to the place where Beppa died."

"That's nice, Honey" Nancy says as she fades back to sleep.

I switch off the iPhone's light, go into the bathroom, brush my teeth, look at myself in the mirror, and think: I've never been back to the Fulton Manor.

SEARCHING SAO PAULO

It was in South America that Garibaldi discovered his true vocation---not as merchant sailor nor as a political conspirator, but as soldier hero.

LUCY RIALL, *GARIBALDI, INVENTION OF A HERO*

SAO PAULO, BRAZIL

When he escaped from Nizza in 1834, Garibaldi made his way to Rio de Janeiro, where, with the help of ex-pat Italians, he earned a living as a merchant seaman. In 1837, he came to Sao Paolo, the capital of the Brazilian Empire, to visit a jailed political prisoner, Bento Conclaves da Silva, the presumptive leader of the breakaway Republic of Rio Grande do Sull. Within weeks of Garibaldi's visit, Conclaves escaped and fled to Santa Caterina about three hundred miles to the south where Garibaldi was waiting with a ship commandeered from the Imperial Navy.

Renamed the Mazzini in honor of his mentor and founder of the "Young Italians," the fledgling republic's first ship of line was manned by a polyglot of volunteers loyal to Conclaves. It is not known whether Garibaldi had any hand in Conclaves' escape but he was soon named Commander of the Rio Grande do Sul Navy, which at the time had a total of two ships, both of which were bottled up in a lagoon that's only access to the sea was blocked by the Imperial Navy. With the help of John Grigg, a young American, Garibaldi transported his two ships fifty miles overland by oxen, and engaged the Imperial Navy in sea battles along Brazil's Atlantic coast.

I'm not sure how it was in Garibaldi's time, but Sao Paulo is big. Big skyscrapers, big limos, big traffic. Big and scary. Streets are crowded and dirty. Graffiti mushrooms well above the third floor on those skyscrapers. John and I walked past one building where it crawled up almost thirty stories. *Did the artists rappel down in the middle of the night, spray cans in hand?* My guidebook says Sao Paulo is the most populous city in all the Americas with about twelve million residents. I wonder just how many of them are actually homeless. Our drive in from the airport yesterday reminded me of scenes of Calcutta. Stacked cardboard boxes and sheets of tin—trashscrapers where thousands live—ran for miles. *How can people live there without it all collapsing?* Half-finished homes—their second floors open to the air—set in residential areas. In the city, high walls topped with barbed wire and cameras surrounded fancy homes.

When we left the hotel this morning the two doormen, dressed to audition for the Blues Brothers, warned us to stick to the main streets of the financial district just two blocks north and *not* to venture in the opposite direction. Along the streets where we're walking we see guns everywhere. Police and security guards tote one on each hip. Every shop entrance we pass has one or two beefy, black-suited sentries with tell-tale bulges under their jackets. *I wonder now many citizens are packin'?* NRA heaven.

We need some local money and figure we'll get a better rate at one of the dozens of banks that line the street. Banco do Brazil looks promising. Two uniformed guards flank the glass-fronted entrance, each wearing aviator sunglasses, trooper hats, two heavy, holstered revolvers, and bandoliers of bullets. *Welcome. We love our customers.* They ignore us as we enter the glass-enclosed lobby where lines of people wait their turn at one of the twenty or so ATMs. Ahead there's another set of glass doors with a sign in Portuguese.

"I think it says something like 'to enter, push buzzer,'" John says reaching for the button.

BZZZZ. We're in. More like a ballroom than a bank with white marble floor, faux marble walls and Venetian plaster. The forty-foot ceiling is hung with alabaster Art Deco chandeliers. In the center stand four lonely teller stations and on the left, a blue-fabric-covered cubical hugs the wall. On either side of it stand hatless, uniformed guards, each wearing a military-style automatic pistol. One of the tellers, an attractive woman in her thirties, beckons us forward. In mangled Italian/Portuguese John explains we want to exchange some dollars.

"*Si, si,*" she answers, then pauses and adds in English, "One moment."

From behind the blue cubical wall a twenty-something Asian woman emerges and click-clicks her way across the floor on five-inch heels. Slender, medium height, with fiery-red hair, she's wearing white Capri pants slung too low, a bright red crop top scooping over a braless chest, and enough gold jewelry to start a revolution. When she asks for our names and passports, John fumbles—for his name.

"How much money would you like to change?" she says, leaning forward slightly. John somehow manages to look her in the eye. She notes his answer on the yellow pad, gives it to the teller and introduces herself: Miko Tanaka, Branch Manager, her manner in direct contrast to her appearance. *This place is giving off some big mixed signals. Palatial interior, heavily armed guards, and now this woman. No bank manager in America would come to work dressed like that. Are we in a real bank or some kind of money laundering scene?*

"You speak excellent English," I say.

"Thank you. Today, in Japantown, there are schools where we can learn Japanese and English. And of course we study Portuguese. There are thousands of Japanese in Sao Paulo. Our people came to work in the coffee fields." She turns to John. "Your name is Italian. Are you visiting relatives here? The city has many residents of Italian descent."

"No," he says, "We're doing research on a book about Giuseppe Garibaldi. Do you recognize his name?"

"Of course. The famous Italian general." John's eyes light up and now he's focused on her face. She points in the direction of the street. "You can find a bust of him in Parque da Luz. His wife, Anita, was Brazilian—from Laguna where my sister lives. The town put up a statue to her in the main square." First impression canceled: This woman is well-educated and accomplished. I guess Brazilian banks care more about what's between your ears than your shirt buttons.

The teller returns with our local money and Ms. Tanaka reaches out her hand. "You ought to go to the Bela Vista neighborhood, the city's Italian section. I'm sure you'll enjoy it," she says. John takes a last look as she clicks back to her office.

Outside, we take her advice and hail a cab to Bela Vista then set off walking. In Garibaldi's day this area was a magnet for Italian immigrants. Today simple facades of yellow, green, blue and orange, reminiscent of coastal Italian towns, line the streets along with theaters, shops, bars and restaurants. At an open-air market we buy a dozen huge purple figs, the biggest I've ever seen, which the vendor packs carefully into an egg carton for us to put in John's backpack. Our meander takes us past Trianon Park, the Vai Vai (Go Go) Samba School, several churches and lots of shops. I want to find some native artwork to take home but everything is slick and manufactured. Then, around a corner, we discover a small street market offering baskets, rugs, and—oh yes!—a colorful, twenty-four-inch papier mache gecko made from scraps by a young man who lives outside the city. He squares his shoulders and a grin crosses his face as he holds it up for my photo. Unfortunately, its tail projects from the backpack quite a bit, almost curling around John's ear.

"Makes me look like a tourist," he grumbles.

"Not a tourist, a nature lover."

Two hours later, we get to Parque da Luz and locate Garibaldi's statue. In our selfie, we're both more tired than the sad face our hero wears. Time to sit, drink and eat.

LOOKING FOR ANITA

Turning his eyes towards Laguna he beheld several pretty young women busy in the household duties of the place. He went thither immediately with a beating heart but firmly bent to his purpose...There he saw a girl whom he liked and said to her "Maiden, you will be mine!"

HOWARD BLACKETT, *LIFE OF GIUSEPPE GARIBALDI, ITALIAN HERO AND PATRIOT*

SAO PAULO, BRAZIL

"What about that place," I ask as we approach an Italian-looking restaurant with outdoor seating.

"Ah, I see why you want to eat here," Nancy says. "The waitress. You think she looks like Anita. Your fantasy of Anita. Right?"

I think to myself. *A winsome eighteen. Short. Athletic. Racially-ambiguous. Alluring. Hmmmm.*

"Well, yeah, she could be Anita. But, look. I'm hungry. The place looks passable. Doesn't it? I'm not looking for fancy. Maybe a sandwich. What do you think?"

Wearing a dark green polo shirt sporting the restaurant's Famiglia Mancini logo, tight dark blue shorts, and a red apron which from the front makes it look like she's wearing a mini-skirt, Anita approaches. In Portuguese she asks *"fora o dentro"* outside or inside. I answer in Italian, *"fuori."*

24

Anita smiles. Understands. Sits us at a table for four next to the street where a dozen motor scooters stand at attention facing us. Another smile. Hands us menus. Walks away.

I am Garibaldi tracking her every move. *Muscular legs. Definitely an athlete. I wonder if she's a horsewoman. It was Anita who taught Garibaldi to ride. Made him a gaucho. Like her father. Converted him from sea captain to a general. During the nine years they were together, they'd ride into many battles. She'd die during their retreat from Rome at age twenty-eight.*

To be fair, the Giuseppe and Anita story comes to us in many forms. For example, authors like Guersoni, Alvensleben, and Jessie White Mario completely deny the fact that when the two lovers met, Anita was already married to Manoel Duarte, a shoemaker and soldier in the Imperial Army. Garibaldi, himself, adds to the confusion by writing in his autobiography "two hearts were joined in an infinite love, but an innocent existence was shattered...I sinned greatly, and I sinned alone." But, he doesn't tell us he took another man's wife. Alexander Dumas' French translation of Garibaldi's memoirs is only slightly less circumspect: "I have found a forbidden treasure, but a treasure of how great a price? If a wrong has been committed, the wrong was mine alone." Or, as Oscar Levant once said of Doris Day: "I knew her before she was a virgin." Mercifully, historians such as Jasper Ridley, Dennis Mack Smith, Howard Blackett, Christopher Hibbet and Lucy Riall paint a much more factual but no less flattering portrait of two people who simply fall in love.

Our Anita returns. "Something to drink?" she says in English. *How did she know we were not locals? Probably the dragon tail.*

Nancy orders an iced tea. I point to the Brahma sign on the window. "*Chopp Brahma,*" I say. Anita smiles approvingly as if to say: Brilliant. He knows *chopp* means draft.

The menu features a variety of Italian/Brazilian dishes including several kinds of barbecued meats, pastas, salads, pizza, and sandwiches. I opt for a prosciutto sandwich—Brazilian prosciutto is not Parma quality but it's certainly better than the Wisconsin prosciutto we get in the States. Nancy settles for a beet salad.

When our Anita returns with our drink and to take our food order, I ask her name.

"Maria," she answers.

I try not to look disappointed.

"Where are you from, Maria?"

"Mexico. Mexico City. I go to University here."

"Wonderful" Nancy says. "You speak English really well. What are you studying?"

"Thank you. Unfortunately, my English is far better than my Portuguese. In school in Mexico I learned English as a second language. Now I'm learning Portuguese. Not so easy. I'm second year pre-med. When I graduate, I hope to attend med school in America." She moves to take an order from another table.

As best we can determine, Anita/Maria is the only outdoor waitress where there are approximately two dozen people occupying about ten tables. She's busy.

Nancy and I share the sandwich and salad but not the drinks.

Anita/Maria returns with a pitcher of tea. As she replenishes Nancy's glass she asks me "Another Brahma?"

"No" I say. "But I do have another question for you? In Mexico, do you study about Giuseppe Garibaldi? Do you know who he is?"

"Of course. Everybody knows Jose Garibaldi, as we call him in Mexico. He was a hero of the Mexican Revolution of 1910. In Mexico City, near my family's home, there is a large square named in his honor. My father plays in a mariachi band; you can find him playing and singing in Piazza Garibaldi almost every Sunday."

"Hero of the Mexican Revolution of 1910. Impossible" I say. "Garibaldi died in 1882."

Anita/Maria looks at me, smiles. "Perhaps, there are more than one."

Ah, there it is. That's what Garibaldi saw as he looked through the telescope from his ship docked off the coast of Laguna. I can see her standing there, chatting with other women. Bang. I could feel it hit him. Italians have a name for it. *Colpo di fulmine.* The thunderbolt. 'Lower the boats; I'm going ashore.'

Impetuous? Obsessive? Quixotic? Before you judge him, consider this. He's been at sea for three years fighting for the break-away republic of Rio Grande do Sol. He's thirty-two years old, in command of two war ships manned by seven Italians, fourteen freed negro slaves—freed by him—two Japanese, three patriots from the Republic of do Sul, and one American—the brilliant twenty-two year old Quaker named John Grigg who captains his second ship. Garibaldi loves his crew members. After what they've been through together, his men would follow him into hell. He and his men are armed to the teeth. So, when he decides to go ashore to look for that woman, that woman with that certain smile, you have to wonder: who's going to stop him?

"Oh, wait," I say, "I believe your Jose Garibaldi was the grandson of Italy's Giuseppe Garibaldi."

Turning to Nancy, I say "Of course. His grandson. His name was also Giuseppe, or Peppino. But Mexicans would have called him Jose. He's Ricciotti's son. Born in Australia. Wounded during WWI. My two uncles served in his regiment. But, I did not know he had also been a hero in Mexico. Damn. A hero of two worlds. Like grandfather; like grandson."

"Isn't this great?" Nancy says. "Ask a question. You never know where it will lead." She already has her iPhone out. Googling: Piazza Garibaldi, Mexico City.

Meanwhile I turn to Maria and say "Maria, I've changed my mind. I'll have that second beer."

It's all there on Wikipedia. Mexican Revolution of 1910. It started when Pancho Villa and Emiliano Zapata, supporters of land reform, challenged the regime of dictator Porfirio Diaz who had defied the Mexican Constitution of 1857 by staying in power for 34 years. Garibaldi Square in Mexico City is named after Lt. Colonel Jose Garibaldi in honor of his heroic actions in the battle of Nuevo Casas Grandes. A nearby metro station off the square also bears his name.

Makes me think about the way history is written. The Civil War. Risorgimento. World War I. World War II. etc. We study them in isolation. Slices of time. Yet, there's a continuum. People. Families.

"Amazing," I say to Nancy. "I knew four of Ricciotti's five sons served in World War I. Two died in bayonet charges. The other two, including Jose, were severely wounded but survived. I wish my two uncles were still alive; I'd love to know their thoughts about Jose.

"How did Rachel Carson put it?" Nancy says. " 'We're all connected.'"

"Precisely," I say. "My uncles served with Garibaldi's grandson. And, every Sunday in Mexico City, Maria's father plays music in the square named in his honor. Talk about six degrees of Kevin Bacon. Perhaps we're closer to the man we're researching than we thought? Maybe only three or four degrees of separation."

"Separation. I'll never forget the story of your two uncles, the way they reconnected in Trieste after the war. What year was it?"

"1918. My Uncle John, Giovanni, was a new eighteen-year-old recruit looking for his older brother camped in Trieste. Giovanni had not seen Antonio for four years. When he tapped an old soldier on the shoulder to ask where he might find Antonio Petralia, the old soldier replied, "I am Antonio Petralia." White-haired and debilitated from four years of tunnel warfare, Antonio was only twenty-two."

"You know, when you showed me the spot at the Port of Trieste where their meeting happened, it was so emotional. Made me cry. That war was so brutal."

"Both my uncles survived to live long lives. But, two weeks after Garibaldi met Anita, his ships were decimated by cannon fire. Garibaldi and Anita survived but most of his men were killed including his great friend, John Griggs. The young Quaker was only twenty two."

Maria is back with my beer. "May I get you anything else?"

"One more question, please, Maria?"

"Yes?"

"Has anyone ever told you that you look like Anita Garibaldi?"

"No. Who was she?"

"She was Giuseppe's wife, Jose's grandmother, a hero here in Brazil as well as in Italy."

"Do you have a picture of her?"

"No" I say. "But, I know exactly what she looks like."

28

SILVER LININGS

The unexpected often tends to happen, sometimes bringing in its train the most delightful change in one's life or circumstances.

ELIZABETH ASTON

BUENOS AIRES, ARGENTINA

In the hired car, on our way from the airport, our first look at Buenos Aires is at night. Traffic is zooming along the broad, crowded highway. In lighted windows of the buildings, I sneak glimpses of Argentinian life.

"There sure are a lot of apartments. It's an enormous city, right?" I say to John.

"I think about three or four million."

"I don't think we're near the city proper yet, but an awful lot of people are living here." Grimy-looking buildings flash by, close to the highway. *Do they have a pollution problem? Maybe this isn't a great part of town?* Many of them look newer, just dirty.

Next to me, my husband is twisting his shoulders right and left trying to loosen his back. It's been a long day for us—up at 4:00 a.m.—and we're both anxious to hit the sheets. Legs achy from hours in a cramped middle seat, I just want to stretch flat on a bed. It wasn't too bad at the airport. Customs checked our passports and visas, took a photo and a thumbprint, and sent us on. I was glad the apartment rental company had arranged our transport so we didn't have

29

to worry about that. *I hope the rental company's timing is right, and that our driver gets us to the apartment on time. We're supposed to meet Miguel at 9:20 p.m.* As directed, we have Uncle Sam's dollars to pay for the security deposit plus our month-long stay. And more for our week in Montevideo. It's tucked deep into John's clothing, but both of us are nervous about carrying so much cash.

Our driver isn't talkative, but then, we can't speak Spanish and he doesn't seem inclined to work with our Italian. When we veer off the expressway and into the city the car stalls at most of the traffic lights, and the driver grinds the gears a few times getting it started again. *Is this guy new on the job?* "Diesel," John says to me. "They stall a lot." I check my watch: 8:50. The driver asks again for the address and we're pretty sure he's lost. After another grating halt he calls someone whose Spanish chatter guides him through the narrow streets. Mid-point in a deserted block he stops—we've arrived. It's 9:10. *I hope the slender young man I can see through the glass front is Miguel.*

He opens the door and greets us in English with a smile and handshake then steers us to the elevator. The door squeaks open revealing a space the size of two phone booths. We all squeeze in—thankful we've brought just two carry-ons and a couple backpacks—for a grinding ride. When Miguel unlocks the door to the apartment there's another man inside.

"The owner," Miguel says. The gray-haired man reaches out a hand and welcomes us in English. He's about six feet with a sturdy build, wearing a faded red shirt and a stubble on his face.

Funny how different things look in photos. I recognize the furnishings, but the room seems much smaller than I anticipated. Dingier too. I remember a nice plump sofa and chair with cute accessories that made it look homey. What I see are worn fabrics, a grimy throw rug, and instead of those cute accessories, a vase of artificial flowers that looks like it might have been here since Garibaldi's days. Miguel shows us to the bedroom—barely enough room to walk around, with grungy outdoor carpeting on the floor. *That never showed in the photo. Can I put my feet on that?* I can imagine what's running through John's head. His face looks as if someone just asked him to clean out the garbage dumpster.

"How does the stove light?" I say when Miguel and I are shoehorned into the narrow kitchen. He turns the gas and nothing happens.

"Use a match," says the owner from the doorway, "or you can get one of those lighters." *Right, none provided.* Miguel locates the matches and a burner flames to life. When we take four steps back to the dining table, Miguel reassures me the wifi is set up. I pull the computer out of John's backpack, set it on the table and boot up. Yes, it's fine.

"We're not staying here," John says to me as we walk back toward the bedroom again. "This place is a dump." A few nights, maybe even a week, we might brave it, eat out and only sleep here. Pretend we're on a CIA stakeout. But we've rented for a month. There's no way we'll be able to stand it that long.

"I'm sorry," John says as we return to the main room, "but we aren't happy. We don't want to stay here. We'll go to a hotel." His words are quiet, but his eyes are hard. Miguel has a distressed look on his face, as if he's realized he's just drunk tainted water.

The owner appears unfazed. He nods, a slight smile on his lips. "It's OK, I can see you aren't comfortable here."

Miguel is flipping through his papers. "That's fine," he says in an officious manner. "But you'll have to pay the cancellation fee."

"How much is that?" John asks.

"Half the rent. $750 dollars US."

"What! We aren't paying *that.*"

"It's in your agreement. If you cancel, you need to pay half."

In what agreement? I don't remember anything about that when I signed up. *This isn't going well. We'll need someplace to stay tonight. Someplace decent.* I sit down and start searching the Internet for a hotel. *Where are we?* I can't recall anything about this neighborhood. There's no time to check TripAdvisor or reviews on Kayak sites. *How will I know if the hotel will be any better than this?* I find something in the general area that looks reasonable.

Over my shoulder the owner's kind voice says, "That's not a good place. The pictures don't show the reality. That photo may look good, but it's not a good hotel." *He ought to know about unreliable photos.* Oh, boy. This is going to be a challenge.

In the meantime John and Miguel are backing into their respective argument corners. "We aren't canceling, Miguel. We just aren't happy with the accommodation. There's a difference."

I'm amazed the owner is taking no offense. In fact, he's being supportive. "I know a good hotel. Very nice. You'll be comfortable there," he says. He tries to find it for me, but I can't read the Spanish site he uses. Finally I manage to get the property on Kayak. Four stars. $169 for the night, plus tax. Not what we bargained for, but at least we'll have a clean bedroom. Fine.

Miguel has now called his supervisor. John is speaking with her. "Miguel has done a fine job...We just aren't happy with this place...Yes, tomorrow... Fine...I'll look for your email." He hands the phone back to Miguel. "She's going to see if she can find something else for us."

John takes his wallet out and gives Miguel the twenty dollars we owe him for our late arrival, plus an extra ten. We thank the owner for his consideration and help with the hotel and cram back into the elevator with Miguel. "Can you help us get a cab, please?" I say when we reach the main floor.

"Sure." He's been professional through it all, played his part, and it's in the hands of his supervisor now. At the door, he pauses. "We have to wait for the owner."

"Why?" I say.

"You need the key to open it."

"From the *inside*? That's scary. What happens if there's a fire?" He doesn't have time to answer as the owner steps out of the tiny elevator, swipes a card at the door, and it unlocks. *Click.* At the street, he takes my suitcase in hand, pulls it to the opposite side and hails a cab for us.

"Thank you," we both say. "You've been very kind."

"It's okay," he says in a reassuring voice, and leans in to give the driver the hotel's address.

Once we're underway I slump down in the back seat and reach over to put my hand on John's knee. "I can't believe how nice he was about it."

"Yeah," John says, his voice weary. "A real gentleman. At least we have a place to stay tonight. We'll worry about another apartment tomorrow."

I look at my watch—10:25. We've been up 22 hours.

Our cab pulls under the two-story portico of LOI Hotel where two husky, black-suited doormen presumably double as guards. The soaring, all-white lobby, with its modern art and vases of exotic flowers, reads high-end boutique. Within a few minutes, we're ensconced in our room—high thread-count linens on the king bed, marble bath, walk-in closet, and small kitchenette with fridge, sink and microwave.

"That's more *like* it," John says, flopping onto the comfy mattress. "Maybe we'll stay another night. It may not be easy to get a new place."

Later when we've turned out the light and spooned together, I think about what's facing us now. "You know, it was almost like what happened when we moved to Italy. Except—thank goodness—this time we hadn't paid for the place yet. How hard is it going to be to find another apartment? The other options on the rental company's website were either unavailable or much more expensive."

He gives me a squeeze. "Right now I just want to get some sleep. Let's worry about apartments tomorrow."

In the morning I draw back the curtains to let in the sunlight. From our ninth story perch I see modern skyscrapers and apartment buildings in the distance. "Look at this," I say, motioning John to the window. "It looks like an old settlement." What appears to be an ancient village, a jumble of gray rooftops, much lower than the surrounding buildings, clusters just a couple blocks away. "We'll have to see what that section is."

Downstairs, we graze the sumptuous buffet in the hotel's glass-roofed atrium. Bow-tied waiters replenish our coffee and refill the food stations with fresh fruit, French pastries, sliced meats and cheeses, eggs, and cereals.

I put my hand over my husband's and gently run my thumb across the top. "A lot better than scrounging around that tiny, awful kitchen this morning."

John takes the last bite of an orange marmalade-topped croissant. "I still can't get over how cooperative the owner was."

"Me either. He sure picked a great hotel for us." Our coffee carafe is empty. *Should I ask for more?*

John pushes his chair back, scraping on the marble floor. "Okay, enough breakfast. Let's take a walk. This neighborhood looks much better than last night's."

Across the street from the hotel's entrance a high, red-brick wall surrounds the block ahead. Poking above it are a few gray steeples and obelisks. We follow along the wall to the gated entrance—Recoleta Cemetery, a Buenos Aires must-see and final home of Eva Peron, Evita. At the sight of the sign my brain clicks a connection. "That must be what we saw from the window this morning! Funny how your eyes play tricks when you're seeing something unexpected. Want to go inside?"

"Let's leave it for another time and go for our walk. Maybe we'll find a place to rent an apartment." *He's right. We have an objective today.* Can't stay in that fancy hotel too much longer.

At the corner we find a multi-story mall, a McDonalds oozing out from the first floor. Ignoring it we follow the streets past small shops and local restaurants. My head is still a bit groggy from the long flight, and it feels good to be out walking in the warm air. Every few yards, we stop to peer into store windows at jewelry, furnishings, pastries, and clothiers, weaving around well-dressed residents hurrying on their own more focused missions. Eventually we come to a large open space where a white-steepled church sits beyond a park and formal flowering gardens.

My attention caught by the reedy sound of a concertina, I locate a red-nosed clown playing under the branches of a low-hanging tree at the edge of the park. "Hey, look over here," I say tugging John toward the tree. Stretched thirty or forty feet across the pavement, the heavy limbs of the sprawling tree are supported by iron braces a foot in diameter. Near the sidewalk edge, a life-size, sculpted man-of-steel shoulders one of the enormous boughs. He's clad in a rough beard and simple loincloth, like a native worker. Unlike me, other sightseers are photographing only the tree.

The white church turns out to be an old Franciscan convent. Inside, behind a quizzical-looking statue of Christ, his arms outstretched in supplication, is a sort of cupboard. Topping five tiers of drawers are three glass-fronted cabinets. The central one reveals the bust of a stricken Mary, her valentine-shaped red heart pierced by a silver knife. On either side, in elaborate silver frames, a human skull stares out over crossbones. *How strange.* In the nave, simple white-painted walls offset polished dark pews and golden altarpieces. *Argento* is the Italian word for silver and there's plenty of it here including an ornate, hammered altar. When I explore a side chapel, and glance out the open window, I'm surprised to see monuments of the adjacent cemetery.

From the church we follow the street down the hill. Happy barking beckons us to where giant fig trees canopy a block-sized park—the apparent meeting point for the city's dog walkers. Protected from the sun, it's cool and dank here and fresh paw tracks cut across thick mud. Clusters of canines, either leashed in groups around the tangled, shoulder-high roots of fig trees, or sitting patiently on a park bench, wait while their minders chat.

"Let's try to find Hotel Alvear," John says when we reach the street of the same name. Our friend Frank had told us he stayed there some years ago in an apartment above the hotel floors. *Maybe we we'll be able to rent one.* I have my doubts when we see the top-hatted, white-gloved doormen and oriental carpet on the entry stairs. Inside a sign declares this "the best hotel in Buenos Aires" and I'm sure it's correct. Old world elegance oozes from the decorative architecture and ornate furnishings. And, no, they don't have apartments. Would we like to book a room? Nightly rate: just under five hundred dollars. "Maybe Frank was thinking of another place," John says as we pass the doormen again.

On a shady block not far away John suggests we try a travel agency. The pretty young receptionist tells us they don't handle rentals, and recommends the company across the hall. There we find a thirty-something man and younger woman who turn out to be English-speakers and siblings—Leonardo and Leti Rapaport. He's a well-built, handsome fellow with close-shaved hair, Italian shoes and engaging manner. Leti's brown tresses form a shallow heart over a high forehead and thick brows. Her smile is infectious.

Yes, they handle rentals, and yes, they've got some places we might like. Leonardo dispatches his sister to show us one nearby. It's okay, clean and well-furnished, but dreary and has a plumbing problem. Back at the office, they make some calls and then Leti takes us in a cab to another. The renovated building, with marble floors and modern furnishings, is trendy and the light-filled apartment comes with the added benefit of a full-time concierge. John tells Leti and the building manager we'll take it.

When we exit John and I decide to walk back to our hotel. I give Leti's slender body a hug. "We'll see you tomorrow at the office. *Molto grazie.*" She starts toward the cross street for a taxi.

"Wait, Leti. Before you go," John says and she returns, "I'm wondering what you know about Garibaldi."

I watch the wheels turning behind Leti's eyes. Surely she considers this a strange question. Then her face brightens. "Yes. I know a Garibaldi. It's a drink, made with orange juice and Campari." She looks puzzled when we both laugh.

"No, *Giuseppe* Garibaldi," he says. "The Hero of Two Worlds. He unified Italy but first he fought here in Argentina. For the Uruguayans." Leti looks embarrassed.

"Don't worry," I say. "He may have been the most famous man in the world in 1860, but today hardly anyone knows who he was." That infectious smile. "Can we get one of those drinks around here?"

"Absolutely," she says gesturing to her left. "You can probably try that place just down the block."

Instead we set off for the Design Center. I've circled it on our city map. Browsing through scads of kitchen displays, tile samples, furniture, and home goods is one of our favorite pastimes. Only a short walk away this one doesn't disappoint. We immediately fall into pointing out things we'd like to have. *Honey, can I decorate an apartment here?* Upstairs, overlooking the park where it's located, are several restaurants and we choose one with an Italian menu posted outside.

Our white-cloth-covered table is near the window where we can watch the people outside. The waiter doesn't speak English, but we choose something we recognize from the menu and get by with Italian. He brings a basket of warm breads and a small dish of a pale yellow substance. There's one medium-grind of pepper across the top.

"Looks like mayonnaise. What do you think it is?" I say. John hates mayo. Won't even taste it.

"Butter? Cheese? Here, try some." He smears a gob on a piece of bread—for me.

The taste is unfamiliar. "It's really good. Not butter though. Not like any cheese I recognize either."

John spreads a piece for himself. "Yeah, it's good." He spreads another larger one. "The pepper punches it up."

When our entrees arrive we ask the waiter what it is. I'm not sure if the look on his face is surprise or irritation. "*Queso*," he says and retreats.

Our familiarity with Latin food is mostly Tex-Mex staples. The *queso* I see in the supermarket is a semi-hard cheese. I never imagined a version like this, creamy and delicious like fresh Italian *burrata*. Our meal, though, is decidedly Italiano: penne with broccoli for John and pumpkin ravioli for me. My Argentinian version, though, has stone-ground mustard sauce. Supple fresh pasta cuddles the squash and the pungent sauce awakens the nose and zings the palate.

John raises his glass, the deep red color catching the sunlight. With the traditional look into each other's eyes, we click *salute*. We survived our first big challenge here—and won. There's a month ahead of us—just the two of us—to explore this gorgeous city. He leans in and whispers. "*Ti amo*," I love you. Already I can feel us drawing closer. I reach across the table, take his hand—the hand I find so beautiful, his strong fingers soft under my touch. Smiling, I spoon a piece of ravioli onto his plate. "You know, I think looking for Garibaldi might be a pretty good idea."

THE FOUR SEASONS

Nature has but a single path and you travel it only once. Each stage of life has it's own appropriate qualities—weakness in childhood, boldness in youth, seriousness in middle age, and maturity in old age. These are fruits that must be harvested in due season.

CICERO

BUENOS AIRES, ARGENTINA

The elevator stops at the sixth floor. We have to walk up the last flight. Standing room only. This is Teatro Colon, Buenos Aires' opera house, where the acoustics are so extraordinary Luciano Pavarotti famously said of the place, "The only thing wrong with Teatro Colon is that when you make a mistake, everyone can hear it." While we would have loved to have heard an opera, this is mid-March; opera season doesn't start until April. Nonetheless, we are about to enjoy a twelve piece chamber ensemble, Camerata Bariloche, led by world famous violinist Freddy Valera Mantera playing the full score of Vivaldi's *Four Seasons*.

The musical ensemble consists of eight men and four women. Save for one middle-aged white-haired man, all the rest, including Freddy, appear to be in their late twenties or early thirties. The men wear white tie and tails; the women shimmer in long tight-fitting white gowns. Attractive, athletic, well lit, they look like Academy award presenters armed with bows.

The music begins with the most familiar of the four seasons, Primavera, Spring. Every note finds me way up here on the seventh floor. If there is an errant bowman, I don't hear him, or her. Somewhere, Vivaldi must be smiling. Me? My mind does what it always does with Vivaldi. It wanders. *Vivace. Allegro.* Playful. It's Spring. Spring, sprang, sprung. *The spring has sprung. The grass is riz. I wonder where the boidie is.*

At the *largo*, the music goes slower, softer. I become more serious, more curious. I'm contemplating construction. No, not how Vivaldi built this music; instead, from my perch on high I'm looking at the theater's structural details. Specifically, the stones. Marbles. Granites. Limestones. All of them. Which ones, I wonder, did my grandfather place in this building? Oh, yes, he worked here. My grandfather, Giuseppe, my father's father, whom I never knew, never saw except in pictures; he took his family here to Buenos Aires from Sicily to work on this building. Maybe he helped construct those grand boxes with their ornate gold filigree? Perhaps the stage? The magnificent entry hall? Maybe, I wonder, he helped construct the very spot where I'm standing? I wish there were some sort of technology that would allow the user to track where a person of interest has been? I bet a whiff of his DNA is here. My grandfather's DNA. I sense it.

I don't know details. I do know my paternal grandfather, a master stone cutter and mason, came to Buenos Aires in 1906 both to flee political oppression in Sicily and to work here, in this building. He was one of hundreds of Italian masons who labored to complete Teatro Colon. The building must contain a million stones. I have no way of knowing which ones he might have chiseled, cut, set or polished. But, whatever parts he worked on, I know they're inside and not outside. By 1906, the exterior—a larger, more-or-less Neo-Palladian construction similar to the White House in Washington, DC—had already been completed. From the street it says big, gray, dull. But, once you enter, the structure intones a distinctive welcome to Italy. White Carrera for the stairway. Reds and pinks from Verona for the balustrades. The tall pink-and-black marble columns are constructed church-like to support the intricately cut mezzanine below me. The shell pattern on the entrance floor, formed with thousands of white marble chips begs the question: How many Italians does it take to make an Argentine heaven?

Our brochure says the theater seats twenty-five hundred people. With the standing room area in the seventh floor, capacity is twenty-eight hundred. Today, the standing room area is full, so is the mezzanine. Down below, at ground level, the high priced subscription seats are only about half filled. I think to myself: a cultural difference. In the USA, in my experience, the rich not only support the fine arts financially, but they'll actually show up for performances.

Premature applause. Unperturbed, Freddy pauses patiently with a nod more grateful than admonishing as he transitions the players to the third movement of Primavera. True to Vivaldi, the pastoral becomes an *allegro ma non troppo*. We're out in the countryside where Freddy switches from performer to conductor. As if a magic wand, his bow draws the sounds from successive violins into birds singing, a dog barking, children laughing. I'm there. Pastoral Sicily, 1906. The have-not Petralia family, has two choices: fight or flight.

This is the dark side of Unification. The part you won't find in the history books.

Following unification, King Vittorio Emmanuel II thanked Garibaldi and then in a "Don't let the door hit you in the ass" moment the self-proclaimed *Father of the Fatherland* bid the old general adieu. Nursing wounds to body and ego, our hero returned to his idyll on the Sardinian isle of Caprera. With Garibaldi out of the picture, the King and his ministers imposed their wills upon their new subjects. First, they confiscated five million gold ducats from the Palermo mint. Then, they seized the national bank of Sicily, killed tens of thousands of armed partisans and civilians, and jailed hundreds on grounds of treason.

Consider this: before the Risorgimento, the two largest and richest cities in Italy were Naples and Palermo, not Rome and Milan. After the Risorgimento, bankrupted Sicily became known, not for its riches and innovative industries, but for its revolutionaries and the Mafia. The entire southern region became the land of the Terroni, a made-up word vaguely translating to dirt-balls—inferior, insolent, indolent, shiftless low classes. Between 1861 and 1906, over a hundred thousand Terroni were murdered or disappeared. Millions of others left for New York, San Francisco, and Buenos Aires.

A stone cutter, union activist, and stereo-typical Terroni, my grandfather was constantly harassed by the police, arrested and questioned for political activities. Concerned for his family, perhaps tired of fighting, he opted to leave. The family would sail to Buenos Aires where Italians, especially skilled Italian stone masons, were welcomed with open arms.

Why Argentina and not the United States? The answer has to do with the times. After the American Civil War, America was expanding rapidly. The country needed immigrants. But, there was also considerable residual ethnic prejudice. Thousands of Chinese, originally brought to the United States to build the railroads, were rounded up and deported. Asians, in general, were not welcome. America preferred Europeans, especially ones from "white" Northern countries. A quota system was legislated. While there were no limitations put on Brits, Irish, Germans, Norwegians or Swedes, there were quotas for Greeks, Spanish, Albanians, Italians and other southern Europeans. In the American South before and after the Civil War, Southern Italians were subjected to the Jim Crow laws. Designated as "black" on census forms, Italians weren't allowed to marry "whites." In 1891, when a Sicilian was accused and then acquitted of killing white New Orleans Police Chief David Hennessy, an irate mob rounded up eleven Sicilians, beat them and hung them in what is considered the largest mass lynching in the United States.

Argentina had no such prejudices, at least not against Italians. Indeed, Argentina was rapidly becoming an Italian colony. The country's climate and terrain are similar to Italy. Today, more than fifty percent of the population owes its origins to Italy. For Nancy and me, Buenos Aires feels far more European than American. With its wide boulevards, green spaces and baroque architecture, it looks and feels like Paris, an Italian Paris to be sure, but just as walkable and exciting. Italian restaurants and Italian names abound. The largest, hippest section of Buenos Aires is called Palermo. Throughout the city, Spanish is spoken with a decidedly Italian accent. Though Nancy and I know little Spanish, most times we are able to make ourselves understood by speaking Italian.

So, when my grandparents selected Argentina as a place to resettle, they were in good company. All aboard! Buenos Aires or bust.

There was one problem. My father, Salvatore, then one year old, had a fever that would prevent him from boarding the ship. To my family, this could mean only one thing: Someone, no doubt a jealous someone, had put an evil eye, the *malocchio*, on the baby. According to Sicilian superstition, anyone can cast the evil eye intentionally or accidentally. It can happen if you pay someone a compliment while feeling jealous or envious. A Sicilian who wants to avoid giving the *malocchio* while paying a compliment might first spit and then say, "Excuse me, I don't want to give the *malocchio*, but your baby is truly beautiful." Jews have an analogous superstition; in Yiddish, it's called *kinahurra*, or the explicit avoidance of talking about something good while it's happening. For example, a knowledgeable Jew might very well say "what a beautiful baby," but that will quickly be followed with the admonition "*kinahurra*," and then spit. Why do Sicilians spit first and Jews second? As Tevye says in *Fiddler on the Roof*: Tradition!

The symptoms of the *malocchio* curse can be moderate to severe including headaches, fatigue and dizziness, or, as in my father's case, high fever. The remedy for the evil eye involves a special ceremony that can only be performed by a widowed grandmother who has been taught the ancient ritual to dispel the curse. As an eleven-year-old in South Philly, I once witnessed the ritual performed on my uncle Giovanni who was suffering from a severe migraine. For some reason, Giovanni's wife, Aunt Jo, thought it would be instructive for me to see how it all worked.

Four of us sat at Aunt Jo's kitchen table: Aunt Jo, Uncle Giovanni, Old Lizzie and me. A widow who lived across the street, and three houses east of us, Lizzie was the grandmother of three "boys" who had served in the U.S. Navy. The youngest, Richie, still lived with his parents and Lizzie in their row home on Sigel Street. Well over six feet tall, straight black hair, handsome, dark like me, good-natured, cool dresser, Richie, not yet twenty-one years old, had already served in the Korean War and was the first guy in our neighborhood to have both an anchor tattoo on his forearm and a convertible. In summer, you could see him cruising around downtown Philly in his souped-up red Ford

Fairlane, top down, usually with some uptown-looking babe riding shotgun. Once in summer, on South 18th Street, while delivering papers on my bike, Richie pulled up to me, top down, stopped, and told the lady next to him to ask me if I had an extra paper for a dollar. I, of course did not hesitate. When that luscious cream pie pursed her lips and said, "Thank you, Johnny," I nearly came in my pants.

With his cars, babes, and attitude, Richie could not have been cooler. Moreover, because we shared the same nickname, there were those who thought we were brothers. When I got into a fight with Billy Castelli, I was told that Billy's older brother, Big Coz, was going to get the kid who bloodied Little Coz's nose. But when someone told Big Coz that Johnny Nigger was Richie Nigger's kid brother, Big Coz backed off. Five years later, Police Chief Frank Rizzo, nicknamed the Cisco Kid, arrested Big Coz on an armed robbery charge. After a six-year prison stint, my guess is Big Coz did not remember me. But, I doubt he ever forgot the pistol whipping he got at the hands of the Cisco Kid.

Shocked by my nickname? What can I tell you? It was the early Fifties. Most kids had nicknames. Coz, Killer, Bear, Pudgie, Fabbsie, Rhino Nose, Chicken Man, Flowers, Bliz, Sharkie, Moose, Dengie. I suppose because we were both dark Sicilians, Richie and I were called Nigger. To be clear, I make no excuses for the past. Times change. I don't use the N-word. And, I don't refer to Italians, including myself, as a wop or dago. All I can tell you is this: in South Philly circa 1951, I loved my nickname.

I'm not sure how old Richie's grandmother was but to me she seemed ancient. Everything about her was morose—black dress, black shoes with two inch heels—like the nuns wore, heavy black stockings, black eyebrows, black mustache, grey hair, sad grey eyes. No matter; Lizzie was Richie's grandmother. Good enough for me.

I recall the ritual like it was yesterday.

On her kitchen table, Aunt Jo places a pasta bowl three-quarters filled with tap water and a saucer containing a tablespoon of olive oil. Lizzie offers a few words of commiseration to both my uncle and aunt. To me, she says nothing.

She's known me all my life but I can't ever remember her ever acknowledging me. I'm invisible.

Lizzie dips her right index finger into the olive oil. She allows one drop to fall into the top of the bowl, "Padre." Another drop to the left, "Figlio." And, to the right side of the bowl, another drop. "Spirito Sancto." These sign-of-the-cross titrations are repeated three times. Staring intently at the oily formations in the bowl, she explains in Italian that if the drops formed one large ball, there is no *malocchio*—something else caused the headache. "Ah," she says. "there are many droplets. They're also moving: A sure sign that "*Qualcuna era invedioso*—someone was envious." Uncle Giovanni was indeed suffering from the *malocchio*. Next, Lizzie's right-hand fingers form the familiar sign of *la corna*—made by the index and little finger extended from a clenched fist in "hook' em horns" fashion. She dips the fingers into the bowl, mumbles something, *Dio Sancto*, something—*Spirito Santo* something—*Gesu Christo* something. More mumbles. She stands, walks to the right of my uncle. He looks up at her. She touches his forehead with her wet index finger, makes a small sign of the cross, then in English says, "You okay now." My uncle seems relieved. My aunt Jo is ecstatic. "Oh, Lizzie, stay for coffee. I have Yum-Yum cake."

In the case of my father's *malocchio* in Sicily, 1906, the exorcism was a bit more complicated—and more dangerous. After viewing the oil droplets, the old widow announced, "Someone has placed something in your well. Until that something is retrieved, I cannot lift the *malocchio*." My grandparents at the time had three other children, my Uncle Antonio who was ten, my Uncle Giovanni —the same uncle Giovanni whom I witnessed having the spell exorcized—who at the time was six, and three-year-old Rosa. Being the right size, gender and demeanor, it was Uncle Giovanni who got the job. After tying him up like a sausage but with both hands free, they lowered him into a deep, black well. The details of the story have been lost over time, but I do know Uncle Giovanni did find and retrieved a rotting piece of meat with sticks penetrating the core. The putrid meat was brought to the old widow. Careful not to touch it herself, she made sign of the *corna* with her index and little finger. She then dipped the horns into the bowl of water and oil, and blessed the meat three times forming the sign of the cross. *"In nome di Padre, Figlio, e Spirito Sancto."* Again, I don't have all the details, but I do know that one week later, the boat sailed for Buenos Aires with the entire family, including my father, fever free, aboard. The opera house in Buenos Aires would be finished and I, one-hundred-ten years later, am here with Nancy to enjoy the *Four Seasons*.

Tango Lessons

There is nothing more notable in Socrates than that he found time, when he was an old man, to learn music and dancing, and thought it time well spent.

BUENOS AIRES, ARGENTINA

Buenos Aires. Home of the tango. The dance of polished intimacy. The dance of feet weaving, or flying, in and out of each other. The dance of kicking heels, twirling legs and tight embraces. The dance of scalding sexuality. Tango. The emblematic dance of Argentina.

The first time I saw a live tango performance was sometime back in the 80's. "Tango Argentina" it was called, and it was the hottest, sexiest thing I'd ever seen on stage. I could feel the heat of those marvelous dancers even up in the mezzanine. I've been dancing since I learned to walk, but tango—tango fascinates me.

Whenever we get the chance to speak with a local I ask, "Where can we see the tango?" Always the reply's a recommendation for a pricey show. The city has scads of them, usually with dinner. Gushing Trip Advisor reviews. But that's not what I'm looking for. I want to see the street dancers. And I want to go where the locals go, to see the ordinary folks dance.

A few days after our arrival in Buenos Aires, John and I have worn ourselves out exploring the streets. "There's a Starbucks," he says with relief, indicating the corner across the street as if it were an apple tree on the surface of Mars.

"You want a Starbucks? In Argentina?"

"I want to sit down. And maybe they'll take my Starbucks card." We cross the street and order. No, they can't take his American card.

"Inside or out?" I say. It's hot, and there's AC inside. I figure he'll want to stay here.

"Outside," he says. *Maybe he's still expecting that apple tree.*

"I'll find a table. You get the coffees."

I commandeer a small table under the eaves and he sets my cappuccino and his regular American down. When I peel off the lid it doesn't look like any cappuccino I've seen. A heap of too-sweet, fake whipped cream on top. Another gob of the whipped stuff floats on his coffee instead of cream. *I guess this is the way the Argentines like their Starbucks.*

Catching bits of conversation around us, we speculate about the speakers. At a table in front, two lanky, chiseled men look like they might be German, our suspicion confirmed by their overloud exchange. At the table behind us, two young women—an American and what seems to be her guide. I've drunk about three-quarters of my coffee when John says, "Look over there. It's a tango studio. Do you want to take some lessons?"

There's nothing I'd like more, and he knows it. Dancing is probably my favorite of the things we do together. We're good, though not conventional dancers. Both of us admire Fred Astaire and Ginger Rogers. No, we can't dance like them, but we're smooth and we get compliments. The best photos of us have always been taken when we're dancing. As if our chemistry comes through and makes the imprint.

But he's never wanted to take a dance lesson.

I look across the street. On the second level, behind a curvaceous iron balcony, arched windows reach the floor. Inside I can see several small slipcovered chairs. Script on the window reads *Estudio de Tango*.

"Sure! Do *you*?"

"We're in Argentina," he says with a shrug. "We might as well."

47

I can't contain my delight.

Embedded in the pavement outside the door is a large concrete slab with footprints of eight numbered male and female steps and the words *Vereda del Tango*, tango path. We ring the bell. A disembodied female voice crackles through the speaker.

"Per lezioni di tango," John says in Italian. She sounds confused, as if his words are in Hindi. He tries again, this time louder. "Tango lessons." The buzzer sounds and we push the door open. Up the curving, heavy wooden staircase, on the second floor we see through more floor-to-ceiling windows. Mirrors line the opposite side of a long, narrow room with crystal chandeliers. When we enter, a woman is busy behind the counter at the rear. "Tango lessons." John says again in English.

"Monday, Wednesday, Friday at eight," she says in Spanish. "Ninety minutes group. Private other times." Back and forth we go in Spanish and Italian to get it straight.

"Wednesday, we will come Wednesday," he says finally.

"Twenty dollars for the two of us," he tells me, shaking his head, as we descend the stairs.

"For a 90 minute class? That's not much at all."

"Maybe we can take several. We'll start with two and see how it goes." I can feel myself smiling, both inside and out. Dance class brings back great memories.

When I was a girl, I took dancing lessons every week. My grandmother would pick me up from school and we'd take two buses to the opposite side of Pittsburgh and Mrs. Fairagreve's Dance School. She seemed old to me, but she was a probably only in her fifties. Her daughter, named Nancy like me, was probably thirty at most. Ballet, tap, modern jazz, and acrobatics. I took them all and loved it. I would bound up the three stories to the studio well ahead of Grandma. When the lessons were over, we'd go to the ice cream store on street level for a hot fudge sundae while we waited for Mom to pick us up.

Each spring, Mrs. Fairagreve put on a recital—but not the kind most dance instructors did. No parents crowded in chairs around the studio perimeter. She rented the thirty-seven-hundred seat Syria Mosque, with an enormous stage and tiered seating just like a New York theater. Each number had its own clever costumes and even props. At the finale, everyone gathered on stage to sing "Give My Regards to Broadway." A real "show." But then, she was the woman who taught Gene Kelly to dance, so she knew a bit about that.

Aside from those special on-stage events, my childhood in the suburbs of Pittsburgh was pretty ordinary. Uneventful. Except for that one time. I was sick. And it was dance school day. Mom insisted I stay home from school and that meant missing dance classes too. I moped around the house sniffling, coughing and eating Grandma's special "invalid" treats—a poached egg on sugared toast drenched in warm milk for breakfast, and warm Jell-O in the afternoon. When Mom came home from work we watched the evening news. The big story was about a building in East Liberty that had burned down in the afternoon. A three alarmer. On the screen firemen doused it with a half dozen hoses while smoke rolled out of the windows like a gaggle of genies escaping their bottle.

"THAT'S MY DANCE SCHOOL!"

Mom scrutinized the screen. "I think you're right," she said with a worried look. When she glanced at me there was relief in her eyes.

Grandma clutched her hand at her mouth. "Oh my. I hope everyone got out."

"And I MISSED it! Why did I have to be *sick* today?" I'd never been so disappointed. Did it happen during my class? How did they all get out? I would have held Grandma's hand as we scurried down the stairs. Would have watched the firemen with the heat on my face and damp cold against my back. Would have seen them haul those giant hoses then struggle to control the spewing torrents. How could I have missed it! Then, I imagined hot fudge seeping out of the doorway on the first floor and pooling onto the sidewalk. *Oh, it would have been wonderful.*

Dance class was cancelled for two weeks until a new location could be found. When we returned we found out that after everyone was out, Nancy had run back up the stairs and gathered together all the sheet music. The school's treasure, it was marked with not just arrangements, but some of the choreography.

49

I jealously thought, at least one Nancy had an exciting day. Would anything extraordinary ever happen to *me*?

Wednesday evening John and I return to dance class. I'm wearing my Mary Jane travel shoes which will slide passably well. John's wearing his soccer shoes. An attractive woman dressed in black slacks approaches us, her dark hair restrained in a tidy, rear knot. "My name is Elsa Maria," she says and gives us both a one-cheek *baci*, the standard Argentine greeting. "I'll be your instructor tonight." No problem, she tells us when we say we've never done the tango before. "You'll learn. Be patient. I've taught many people. Where are you from?" When we tell her America—Philadelphia and Florida a wistful smile crosses her lips. "A long time ago I worked in New York. I was in Tango Argentina on Broadway, then on tour."

"Really? I must have seen you!" I say. "That was an amazing show. I still remember it."

"Yes—and then I became a teacher." Behind her on the wall hangs a collection of photographs. "We'll get started in a few minutes." She gestures toward the white-draped chairs. "Take a seat."

For now the pictures will have to wait.

We head toward the cluster of ivory-slipcovered chairs in the back of the room. Three people are seated already—a twenty-something girl, a man about the same age, and an older one, all locals. We introduce ourselves and each gives us the one-cheek kiss. We learn the two men are father and son. While we talk the three of them are donning fancy dancing shoes. A mature woman soon joins us and pulls out her strappy high heels.

"Elsa Maria is quite famous," the older man says as he ties a lace. "She was with Tango Argentina, and a teacher of many famous people—Sinatra, Simon Peres, Al Pacino—"

Al Pacino? I'll never forget that scene in *Scent of a Woman*. Al Pacino plays a blind man who dances a sensuous tango with a beautiful young woman. I love that scene, the best one in the movie. Elsa Marie taught *him*—and now *we're* going to take lessons from her. What a lucky stop that Starbucks turned out to be.

As the eight o'clock hour approaches the last two arrivals cinch on dancing heels. Dim lighting in the long, narrow room never changes. Plaster decorations embellish the ceiling. Everything is soft, worn, white like an old satin ball gown. Elsa Maria leads us to the parqueted dance floor. A recording starts and she takes us through some warm-up steps. Side to side, back and front. A few others have materialized in the group. Slowly, she demonstrates the basic steps. I can follow that. Next the man's part, almost the same. Now the position—back straight. His right hand on my back. Lead with the fingers and palm. *Not so easy. He doesn't lead like that. We don't dance like this.* We're bumbling around, but unfazed.

It gets harder. There's the turn step. I turn back and forth while he stands and guides me with his right hand, pressing fingers for the left, palm for the right, three or four times. Then, the resolution, and start over. We get it all mixed up, tangle our feet together, and I turn the wrong way. Was I this gawkish in my childhood dance classes? *Patience she'd said.* We keep trying. By the end of the class we have a clumsy comprehension of what we're supposed to do.

Before we leave I take a look at the photos. The woman in them is in her thirties and drop-dead gorgeous with chin-length black hair and bangs, bright red lips, dangling earrings and sequined gowns. There she is with Sinatra, Peres, Liza Minnelli and Placido Domingo. A dancing pose with Robert Duval, who I know to be a great tango dancer. On the opposite wall are several photos of Elsa Maria with Bill and Hillary.

"You taught Bill Clinton the tango!" I say as we head for the door.

"It was only a few minutes," she says nodding. "But a nice experience." One of many I imagine.

As we turn to leave John says, "We'll see you again on Friday night, *Buona notte.*"

"We should practice," my husband says the next day. But instead we take a walk.

Buenos Aires is full of beautiful parks, quite a few close to our apartment, with museums set in several. Our rental agent, Leti Rapaport, spurred by our interest in Garibaldi, has suggested we meet her father. "He speaks English and loves history. I think he'll be able to talk with you about Garibaldi." At noon, we'll meet the two of them for lunch at Croque Madame next to the Decorative Arts Museum.

This morning, we've decided to explore the area along Avenue del Libertador, the wide boulevard in front of the museum. It feels like Paris with ten lanes full of taxis, cars and speeding buses heading north. To avoid death-by-auto, everyone crosses with the light at the corners. Along the street, as if by some English monarch's decree, manicured gardens green the fifteen feet between the wide pavement and the avenue in front of each building. Five-story trees spread their leafy arms over pedestrians mitigating the blazing heat. Huge, polished, wooden or brass doors lead into the apartment buildings, many with glass walls on the first level, through which we glimpse marble lobbies, and modern sculptures inside. On a corner we pass the Italian embassy with its unmistakable *punti*, cherubs, playing on a frieze and across the roof.

A block east Avenue President Figueroa Alcorta runs the opposite direction. The area around it must be the ultimate apartment address. Fashionable buildings line both sides of the boulevard with huge shade trees and more English-style gardens next to the street. We slip into what we think is a luxury shopping mall and stroll down the marble hall to where we can see a treed courtyard. Sleek, white lounge chairs line a long lap pool. At the sound of footsteps hurrying toward us, I snap a photo just before the door guard catches up. "This is a private building," he says. "You will have to leave."

Beyond Alcorta we discover a residential section of embassies and exquisite homes. None higher than three stories, the styles range from Tudor stone-and-brick, to iron-balconied Spanish and French, to Mediterranean white with polished wood doors and shutters, to ultra modern glass and wood. Security stations, looking like over-sized phone booths, and plenty of black-suited men with guns leave no doubt who lives here.

Returning to the Croque Madame at noon, we meet Leti and her father, Bernardo. Stocky and round-faced with receding gray hair, he has an impish smile and enthusiastic manner. His English is excellent, like his daughter's. He tells us he owns a small business here and is still working—but only so the family can travel. They'll be going to Europe, Turkey and the USA in the coming months. "What do you think of Buenos Aires?" he asks over our lemonade and iced tea.

"It's a gorgeous city. I love all the parks, and the trees here are magnificent. There's so much shade in the city," I say. "Yesterday, when we were downtown, there was a jazz band playing on the street corner that could have been in a concert hall. And we enjoyed the art market on Saturday." Leti echoes my enthusiasm for the art market and shopping for casual jewelry and leather goods there.

Our salads arrive, each topped with chicken or beef. "Rapaport is a Jewish name. How did your family come to Argentina?" John asks Bernardo as we're eating.

"Our name comes from the original Askenasic name Rapa coupled with the town, Porto, Italy. My ancestors settled there when they fled political persecution in Odessa a hundred years before. They lived in Italy until my grandfather brought his family to Argentina. My wife's Catholic and half Italian. Her Italian grandfather did the same."

John says, "Must have been around the time *my* grandfather came here."

"People came here from all over. In Buenos Aires you'll find lots of Italians, Spanish, English, Germans and Irish. Like America, it's a meld." He takes a few bites of his lunch. "Have you been to the cemetery yet?"

"We have," I say. "We went a few days ago. Saw Evita's grave of course, but I found all of it fascinating. More like a sculpture garden in places."

"Did you see the tall, green obelisk near the center?"

I'd read up on the cemetery before we went. Several of the deceased had a connection to Garibaldi, and we'd tried to find all the most famous memorials. That obelisk was among them. "Yes, we did," I say. "Admiral Brown. He was Irish, so it's painted green and I read they melted some of the cannons from his old battleships for the mausoleum."

Bernardo seems pleased we bothered to find out. He says, "Admiral Brown was one of the heroes of the fight for Argentinian independence. After the war, he and many others stayed." The two men spend the next few minutes talking about Argentinian history. It turns out Bernardo doesn't know much about Garibaldi, but, after all, Garibaldi was the enemy in the fight with Uruguay.

"Our first day we walked up to Plaza Italia. There's a magnificent statue of him here," I say sipping the iced tea that cools my throat. "And in such a prominent spot. That surprised me."

Bernardo nods. "It was given by the Italian-Argentinian people. You'll find many tributes to foreigners around the city."

We've noticed that. In addition to Plaza Italia, we've seen Plaza Francia and streets named Paraguay, Honduras, Chile, El Salvador, Guatemala, and Costa Rica. Even Estados Unidos, United States. Our apartment is on the corner of Austria.

Leti excuses herself to return to work while Bernardo leans across his empty plate, eager to pass on things we shouldn't miss—San Telmo, the craft market near the cemetery, the museums, including the one next door. As we're sipping our coffee he asks what we have planned for the rest of the day.

John says, "We'll visit the Decorative Arts after lunch, then probably take a rest. We have our second tango lesson tonight."

"You're taking tango lessons! Impressive." He gives a short hand clap. "It's difficult."

"We figured that much out already," I say with a laugh. "A fellow in our class said learning was a right of passage for young men. That fathers taught their daughters to dance, but the young men had to learn on their own."

"True," Bernardo says. "Italian immigrants created much of the music, influenced by their native folk songs and tarantellas. The dancing started with people from the countryside, and sailors coming into town to visit the hookers. They had great expectations. But mostly they were disappointed. Women wouldn't look at them unless they could dance. And so they watched, and watched, practiced and danced with each other until they had the courage—and the skills—to ask a woman. All of that is reflected in the music."

In my head, a mournful violin is playing. "It's such beautiful music. Sad and melancholy and longing. It pulls on your heart like opera."

"Tango's not easy to master. Good luck with your lessons," Bernardo says. He pushes his chair back and picks up his cap. "Before you leave for home, I'd like you to meet my wife. She doesn't speak English, but she understands Italian. Let me know when we could have coffee together. And if you need anything, send me an email."

Waving to our new friend, we're off to see the Decorative Arts Museum next door. A prominent family built their retirement home on this avenue just before the first World War. Like mansions of American's wealthy industrialists built around the time, it mimics European noblemen's residences. The multi-story Great Hall could be in a castle in Italy, England, or France with enormous tapestries hung on two walls, the ballroom a scaled-down Versailles. With its sumptuous furnishings, paintings and sculptures—including El Greco, Manet, and Rodin—it's more residence than museum.

Hours later we ring the bell at the dance studio and climb the curved wooden staircase to the second floor. Like the last time, the room's dim light comes from three crystal chandeliers. None of the students from Wednesday are here tonight, and neither is Elsa Maria. When we ask, we're introduced to tonight's instructor, a former ballerina named Martina. Her body, in black spaghetti-strap top and silky, teal pantaloons gathered at her ankles, is still youthful. But she wears seventy years on her face. It's still lovely with high cheekbones and dramatic eyes. Long hair, a color somewhere between magenta and burgundy, is piled above her slender neck. She gives us a cursory acknowledgement and glides to the floor.

The students line up behind her for a warm up. It's different from Elsa Marie's. Her body, held by an invisible string, is perfectly erect. Her foot slides quickly to the right, to the front, just like the basic ballet steps I recall from my childhood. She's speaking rapid Spanish about I-don't-know-what, so I concentrate on her feet. *Good. I'm able to follow.*

The door flies open and a man in his fifties rushes in, tosses his black cap onto one of the tables, and joins the floor. Carlo, the other instructor, someone says. Dressed in black pants, his white shirt open at the neck, he's got a husky build and ready grin. Our warm-up complete, it's time to dance. Martina and the new man demonstrate.

Uh-oh. We look at each other in dismay. "I thought we'd get a little better at that basic step," I say to John. "This is a totally different sequence from Wednesday night."

"Let's just try it," he says, reaching out his arms. Together we attempt to mimic our instructors. It's not going well. I keep getting my feet mixed up and he's not moving in the right direction. Apparently the other students have done this before as they're moving around the floor with decent grace. Carlo steps in and works with John on the steps then takes my arms and leads me pressing my back with his fingers and guiding with his shoulders. After a few tries I manage to get it. Back together with John, we lurch our way around the floor.

Now Martina takes charge of me. I'm not crossing my left foot properly. In rapid Spanish she's explaining something. *"Non parlo spangolo,"* I say in Italian. I don't speak Spanish. It doesn't seem to matter. She keeps right on talking while snapping her left foot across her right. From the demonstration I figure out I'm supposed to shift my weight once this is done. That's not working so well. I feel like a hobbled chicken struggling to get free. Martina, on the other hand, moves gracefully on her toes and slides into the next step. After several tries her frustration is apparent. Still rattling in Spanish, she reaches out and pushes hard on my knee. Bend! I remember the *plié* from dancing school. *It was so easy then.* Turn your toes out and bend your knees. That was about fifty-five years ago. I'm trying, but my knees aren't cooperating. Martina keeps insisting and *pushing.*

"Mi dispiace. Le mie ginocchia sono vecchi." Sorry. My knees are *old.* Martina gives me a look. Right, it says—old because you haven't continued to dance. Her kind of dance. Now I do plenty of dancing, just not the kind where I have to bend my knees and shift. *You should see my Mashed Potatoes. I can twist my ankles and knees all night long. I'll bet you can't do that.* But that's not the point, so I tuck my bruised ego away and try again. A little better.

"Isn't this over yet?" I whisper to John when we're together again. "My knees are killing me. Hips too. I can't wait to get an Aleve."

His face is moist and his hands clammy. "It's so hot in here," he says. "Let's move under the fan." Its slow turn barely disturbs the air. "That's a *little* better."

When we've completed the steps a few more times, I feel more confident about it. "I think we're getting the sequence, now. We aren't too bad."

He lifts my chin, looks in my eyes. "We're perfect. *You're* perfect."

Tango lessons. A gift of love.

I've read about the *milonga*—a place where locals go to dance. We'd like to find one, but how? I forgot to ask at the dance studio. Downstairs in our apartment building the next morning I ask our concierge, Marco, where the locals go. He pulls out several brochures for dinner and tango shows.

"No. Not a professional show, Marco. We want dancing by real folks." Marco is stumped.

Tongue firmly in cheek, John says, "Now that we've had two whole lessons, we're ready for the dance floor."

From the open door of the office, Scott joins us. He's the building owner and an American. On our first night, he gave us good advice about the Italian restaurant down the street. He says, "There's a good place in Palermo. Upstairs is an Armenian restaurant. Go there for dinner—the food is terrific. Downstairs in the basement is the *milonga*."

"Armenian! I love Armenian food. What time should we go?" I ask.

"Probably around ten or eleven would be good. Reserve a table. They give a lesson and a chance to practice before the real dancing starts." He takes a card from the counter, scribbles La Virtua Tango on the back, and I tuck it securely into my purse.

"How about a demo?" Marco calls as we head for the door.

"Not yet," John replies over his shoulder, "we've got a long way to go."

On Friday night at nine, we take a cab to the Armenian Cultural Center near Piazza Armenia. A nondescript building, its first floor lobby has a case full of soccer trophies. Upstairs the restaurant is empty except for two tables. Our waiter, who turns out to be German, speaks English and recommends the assorted appetizers to precede our shish kebob. When he brings the tray a short while later we understand why there's a smaller table attached to ours. The plates fill both of them. Fresh-made hummus, falafel, marinated eggplant with raisins and almonds, chunky tabbouli and slices of dried pork. A meal in itself and scrumptious. The lamb shish kebob is tender and a welcome change from all the beef we've been eating. Closer to ten o'clock the room is filling up with groups of women, couples, and parties of families or friends. A few minutes before ten John waives at our waiter with no success. When he arrives later with the bill he counsels us to wait for the dancing which is about to start.

A young couple huddles next to the long bar. She wears a simple white blouse and dark skirt and he's dressed in a dark shirt and pants. They're fiddling with a large, red handkerchief. I say to John, "Do you think they're the dancers? She looks like one of the waitresses."

"Could be." He scans the room. "I don't know what's happened to our waiter. I'd like to get my card back and get out of here." Minutes pass and he's nowhere to be found.

A lively drumbeat swells across the room. It's joined by a reedy sing-song tune that could be coaxing a serpent from a basket. In the modest space near the bar, the young couple join hands, he twirling the red handkerchief, and begin a hopping step. We can't see their feet, but from the bouncing, I can imagine the steps of a folk dance. Up and back, round in a circle they bound, then leap, kicking feet high in the air. When the girl takes a turn on her own, she twirls clapping over her head and the now full room comes alive clapping in accompaniment. His turn next. They join hands again and start it all over. *This is fun, but where's the waiter? We need to get downstairs.*

Finally the dance is over, the bouncing couple retreats to the back of the room, and John finally is able to flag down our server. As he's tucking the card into his wallet my husband says how much we enjoyed the dance. "There's much more coming," says the waiter.

"I'm sorry, but we want to get downstairs for the tango," I say, gathering up my tiny purse and smiling to cover my hasty retreat. The server gives us a nod and returns my smile with a wry one.

"Enjoy yourselves," he says as we hurry to the door.

The basement atmosphere makes me think of a speak-easy. Two attractive young women greet us at the bottom of the stair. When we mention our reservation, one of them checks her list then leads us to a table—at the edge of the dance floor. "That was ten dollars well spent," I say, taking my seat which has a clear shot of the dancers.

Tables are jammed four deep around the dance floor which is about the size of a basketball court. Those who didn't reserve a table are seated at a bar along the rear wall or gathered in clusters around the room. Three couples are sliding their way across the floor in smooth, polished tango. The women occasionally kick up their heels as they weave in and out of the men's feet in time with the slow, passionate music.

"Wow, this is so fabulous. Just look at them."

Across the table John nods. "Happy?"

Leaning forward I'm focused on watching the feet. "You bet." Excitement, curiosity, and my dancing feet make me feel thirty years younger, as if I'd once more stepped into the basement rehearsal hall of the Syria Mosque.

A moment later the music ends and applause thunders through the room. Colored light now streaks blue and red across its floor. One of the dancers, a forty-something man with a longish crewcut, steps into the middle of the room and speaks a few words. Then the music starts again, but this time it's a lively salsa. The dancers prance gracefully around the floor to the new beat as the crowd claps with the music. *What happened to the tango?* After three short demonstrations, the MC takes the floor again. But this time, when the music restarts, it's Little Richard's "Long Tall Sally." He twirls a young woman in a kicky, short, white dress through a lively jitterbug, then twirls her again into the arms of a young man. Together they rock through the end of the song to huge applause. Another jitterbug demo and then the MC explains about the dance lessons they give here, pointing to opposite ends of the floor where they'll take place—beginners near the bar and more experienced dancers next to the bandstand.

I can't believe this. "We *missed* the tango demo—for Armenian folk dancing!"

"Come on, let's give it a try." John takes my hand and we join a crowd of others near the bar. Two of the demo dancers are explaining the step. It's the basic one we learned from Elsa Marie the first night, so I'm happy we aren't completely clueless. They separate us into two lines—men on one side, women on the other—and slowly go through the pattern. Over the music I can barely hear our young instructor's words, but she's talking in Spanish so it makes little difference. She's easy to follow, though, moving slowly and deliberately over and over the basic feet positions. On the opposite side, her partner is doing the same with the guys. I remember that somewhere on their website I read they also speak English. So just as we're being told to find a partner, I tap my instructor's shoulder and ask her to explain the cross and weight-shift that troubles me so much. Sure enough, she does—in the language I can understand—with no pushing on my knee.

Now it's time for us to try it together. Both of us are feeling more confident than any prior time and indeed we manage the little routine several times before we're told to change partners. In the next few minutes John takes a pretty girl in his outstretched arms and I, polite and apologetic, stumble through a short dance first with a geeky-looking fellow and then with a chubby one. Like everything in married life, you get used to the feel of your partner. These new ones, especially since neither of us is dancing well, feel especially odd. I'm glad when John and I find each other for a few more circles around the floor. And then the lesson's over.

As we walk back to our table, he says, "We did pretty well. I think we'll be able to dance once the real thing starts."

"Maybe." I'm dubious, but willing to try.

Before long the lights go down, leaving only the colored spots. The melancholy music begins. Couples rise from the tables and barstools and slip onto the dance floor. In a moment it's full. A few of the men, dressed in soft leather shoes and the loose-fitting pants favored by Gene Kelly, are obviously showing off their talent, gliding their partners flawlessly around the floor. Most of the women are in dresses, and all are wearing heels. But whether in fancy dress or everyday, these are *dancers*. No halting steps, or squashed toes. No bumping into others on the floor. They sweep counter-clockwise round and round weaving in and out without effort.

"Think we'll ever be able to do that? I can't even follow their steps." I say.

"Let's give it a try," He slides his chair back and takes my hand. Reluctantly I follow him onto the edge of the floor where we take our start pose and walk through the basic steps. Others glide past us. We get it wrong and try again, bumping into someone. Hugging the edge of the floor, we persevere to the end of the song while young and old glide gracefully past us.

I recall Bernardo's story of the sailors dancing together to perfect their skill. "Let's just watch," I say when we're seated again. "I think you have to be reasonably good to be out there."

Looking into my eyes, John gives my hand a squeeze. "You're fabulous," he says.

Tango is a dance you do at your own pace. Some couples slide by in long, graceful steps moving quickly across the floor. Others, moving in half-time—almost slow-motion—their feet passing within a hair of each other. His legs wrapping round her, her heels slowly kicking then slithering behind his ankles as if making love. Although the ladies are the showiest, mostly it's the older men who are the best. Many appear to be without a steady partner and so guide a supple young woman through a single dance, then select another. For those few minutes, age and status disappear and both are transported with the music and movement. *That scene in Scent of a Woman. How could a blind man do that? Because it's a dance of feeling, not seeing.* Many of the dancers move about the floor with closed eyes.

Mood shift. The loudspeaker blares a jitterbug and on the dance floor, the couples change. Swinging, with feet shuffling and hopping, they're all pretty good—but I can't take my eyes off the couple to my right. He's quite tall—dark hair combed back and a swarthy complexion, his features a mix of European and native—and stunningly handsome. Dressed all in black, wearing the softest, thinnest shoes, his body is muscular yet flexible as a slithering snake—a *dancer*. She's a head shorter in a black lace, swingy skirt and top, her blonde hair flinging across her shoulder blades. She's not just cover girl beautiful, but a terrific dancer. Together they put on a show worthy of Broadway. *Are they professional dancers?* Moving three times as fast as the demo couples, they kick and shuffle and twirl and laugh, having a great time. When the music changes again, this time to salsa, they give us another show. At the end of the set they drift off the dance floor and I see them with a group near the wall in the back. I'm hoping they'll dance in the next tango set. But when it comes up, each of them is with a different partner—he with another young woman, and she with an elderly man who's maybe as talented as she.

This is why we wanted a *milonga*. Ordinary people dance here. They go, not just for tango, but for salsa, and rock 'n' roll. Tango, though, is a form of sexual play for young and old. A way of feeling vibrant and alluring. This is a place where older folks with skill out-dance young ones. A place where younger ones come to learn. On the dance floor people of all shapes, sizes and ages are welcomed and accepted. Sort of like this country.

At around midnight the band starts to set up but the canned music is still going after one. I could watch the dancers all night, but John's looking tired.

"Let's go," he says. I can tell by his tone he's serious.

"Can't we stay until the band starts? We've waited this long and they seem to be getting ready to play. Just a little longer, okay?" He gives me one of his just-for-a-while looks and settles back in his chair.

Finally the bandstand lights go bright and acoustic guitars, horns and a red accordion swirl the room with a rapid tango. Dancers hurry to the floor. At the end of their number John pulls me toward the door. I'm tired too. It's nearly two a.m. We haven't been out this late in years, even on New Year's Eve. Reluctantly I climb the stairs. *Oh, to be young and in Argentina.*

Next morning I have to tell Marco. "How was the dancing?" he asks when we approach the counter. He's probably about twenty-seven, large dark eyes, slender and handsome, outgoing and competent.

"Terrific. Mostly we watched, but it was wonderful. Do you tango, Marco?"

He looks shy, as if I've asked him if he sleeps with his girlfriend. "No. I like to watch it, but I don't tango."

"You need to learn. There were lots of young men about your age in our lesson. And some very talented ones on the dance floor. No one makes you feel uncomfortable. Besides, it's part of your culture." *What am I doing lecturing this courteous young man on his culture!*

He gives me a weak smile and says, "Maybe one of these days."

"Maybe one of these days *we'll* be able to do it," John says.

"I thought last night's lesson really helped. We got the basic down pretty well. See you later, Marco, we're off to the art market today."

When we're out on the sidewalk John takes my hand. "When we get home, maybe we can find a place to take tango lessons." Then he pulls me into his arms and guides me through the basic movement, turns gracefully and starts again.

The feeling in my heart is warmer than a hot fudge sundae.

MAGICAL REALISM

Reality leaves a lot to the imagination.

JOHN LENNON

BUENOS AIRES, ARGENTINA

The hostess here at Clark's Steak House has my attention. Late twenties. Auburn hair. Blue eyes. Medium height. Gorgeous figure. Alluring smile—with a distinct difference: Deep scars that slice her lower lip and left cheek. I am trying hard not to stare. She's taking us to a booth in the rear section past a long bar.

As she's seating us, she asks in English "Are you Americans?"

"Yes."

"Oh, I love the United States."

"You've been?" I ask.

"Yes, once. One week only. Las Vegas. Two years ago. With my boyfriend, Duncan. He's an engineer. We went to a convention. Stayed at the Venetian which was fabulous."

"Ah, yes," Nancy says. "I've never been but I hear it's a beautiful place."

"You know, I have to tell you," the hostess replies, "Last year, we went to the real Venice. Didn't like it much. Very dirty. Too expensive. So many tourists." Laughing now, she adds, "Honestly, I much preferred the Venice of Las Vegas."

Nancy and I are not totally surprised. Venice—the one in Italy—happens to be our favorite place in the whole world. For us, Venice is pure magic. We've been several times and plan to return. But, we know Venice can be daunting. A few years ago, one of our relatives planned to stay two weeks and left after two days; she said the place made her sick. Perhaps she should have gone to the Las Vegas Venetian first for a test drive.

"So, you're tourists?"

I think to myself. *Hold on there, lady! Don't stereotype me. Do I need to show you reviews of our last book to prove we are writers?* "No. We're here on business, doing research for a new book." *Take that.*

It's 8 p.m. There are only a few patrons. Probably tourists. Argentines don't eat before 10:00 p.m. Matilda—that's her name—has time to chat. A native of Buenos Aires with parents of both Spanish and Italian origins, she speaks seven languages (count them) including Italian and English. Because we're tired, our choice is English.

We ask if she knows about Garibaldi?

"Oh, we serve a great Garibaldi here. Want to try?"

When she sees a knowing smile pass between us, she goes on. "You do know a Garibaldi is currently one of Buenos Aires' more popular drinks? Here at Clark's we make it with Campari, vodka and orange juice; served over ice; it's quite refreshing. Want to try?"

"I suppose we should. Perhaps after dinner. What about Garibaldi the historical figure? What do you know about him?"

"Ah, the man! Everyone in Buenos Aires knows the large statue of him in Piazza Italia. Very impressive. We know he's an important Italian, a historical figure, but not much else. Sorry to say—to me, Garibaldi is a cocktail. Why is he famous?"

"He's known as the Hero of Two Worlds" I say. "A freedom fighter both for South America and Europe. You should check him out on the Internet."

Matilda smiles that smile, and says, "I'll do that. For sure."

As Matilda walks away to greet other patrons, I say to Nancy: "She reminds me of Garibaldi."

"Anita?"

"No, Giuseppe. It's that scar. Garibaldi had a scar on his left cheek. A present from an Argentine war lord. Remember, I told you about it."

June 15, 1837. Garibaldi was captaining a war ship for the break-away republic of Rio Grande do Sol. Unbeknownst to him, Uruguay briefly entered the conflict on the side of Brazil. (I know! History is complicated.) Two Uruguayan cutters engaged Garibaldi in battle. He was struck down by a bullet to the neck. With their captain on the brink of death, the crew members of the Farronpilha put into the neutral Argentine port of Gualeguay, about one hundred fifty miles west of Buenos Aires. After surgery and several weeks of recuperation, Garibaldi was brought before Gualeguay's military commander, Leonard Millan. Millan decided this glory-seeking Italian interloper needed to be taught a lesson. He had Garibaldi stripped to the waist, hung by his wrists, and horsewhipped to within an inch of his life; then he threw him in jail. Only through the intercession of an influential admirer, was Garibaldi released in March 1838.

"Brutal experience," Nancy says.

"Yes, but, that scar gave him—what to call it?—you know, that certain *je ne sais quoi*. Like our young hostess there."

Call it charisma. Sex appeal. Garibaldi had it. Throughout his life, women chased him. Aristocrats like the Englishwomen Jesse Mario and wealthy widow Emma Roberts; and his German biographer, Maria Von Schwartz. Indeed, the person who had arranged for his release from Millan's clutches was a woman from Buenos Aires, Madam Alemain. We don't know much about her or how she and Garibaldi knew each other. In his memoirs, Garibaldi avoids discussions of affairs outside of his marriages—except for Alemain—whom he calls "my beautiful angel of mercy, the one woman I'll always love."

I can't help wondering about Matilda. *How about it, young lady? Do your scars come with a story? Did a jealous lover cut you with a broken bottle? Were you caught in barbed wire during an escape from captivity? Have you thought about plastic surgery? Or, do you find the scars give you a certain élan. You don't seem the least bit self-conscious about them in any way. Good for you. Wear them with pride. Scars didn't stop Garibaldi.*

When Matilda returns, Nancy asks her. "Do you know of the famous Italian woman, Princess Matilda Di Cannosa, the Defender of the Faith? She lived in the twelfth century and was not only a great general but is said to have founded more than a hundred churches throughout the Italian peninsula." No she doesn't know.

Whatever her history, our Matilda has a job to do. She introduces us to an unscarred middle aged waiter in a white jacket who hands us a menu, bows, disappears, returns. We order.

Over the bar, the TV blares away. The news looks like trailers from a series of disaster films. In the southern part of the country, floods have displaced nearly a half million people. Boats are maneuvering though crowded streets of Santa Fe rescuing stranded residents. A camera pans in on a brown-and-white beagle barking alerts from the second story porch of a red brick house still managing to hold its ground against rushing black water flooding the street. Is this New Orleans or Argentina?

To cover both tragedies simultaneously, the TV goes to split screen. The other half of the screen shows forest fires out west. I can decipher only some of the interview with a fire chief; he's concerned his helicopters won't be able to drop a sufficient number of water bombs before nightfall.

Ordinarily we avoid any type of eating establishment where TV is the main attraction. However, two things were different this time: rain and weariness. After a full day of trekking around Buenos Aires in the rain we were too tired and too wet to venture far from our apartment. Moreover, both our desk clerks, chatty Marcella and serious Marcella, recommended Clark's as a "must."

Sitting here, warm and dry, now enjoying a pit roasted steak served with a peppery cream sauce and a side of fluffy white rice, I know we've made the right choice. As I make the rice more risotto-like by mixing excess sauce with it, I say to Nancy, "Aren't you happy we listened to the Marcellas and came here?" Instead of answering, she clicks her wine glass against mine and returns to her dinner: Clark's *bife de chorizo*, steak, served with French fries. Without asking permission, I take a sip of her wine, the house Malbec. Acceptable, but my Paul Hobbs Malbec is far superior. Atypical of us, we decided to limit our wine intake tonight to one glass each. No restrictions on water; we each have a liter (you read that right) of sparkling water.

It's pushing 9 p.m., still too early for dinner in Buenos Aires. Only three of the thirty or so tables are occupied. Nonetheless, halfway into our meal, Matilda escorts a young couple to the table next to us. The new arrivals overhear our conversation about the two disasters on TV. The young man turns to me and says in English, "You can be sure the opposition will blame Kirchner for these troubles as well."

It takes one or two beats for me to get it, but I'm there. He's talking about Argentine president, Christine de Kirchner.

"Blame her for the fires or the floods, or both?" I say.

"Since it can't be climate change causing any of this it must be Kirchner; right?"

I laugh, "And, I thought the global warming deniers were only in America."

"Oh, in Argentina, doubt is our middle name," he says.

"Must be contagious," I say. "So, I need to ask you. Do people here deny that Kirchner had Nisman killed?"

I'm referring to the big story in Argentina. The so-called Nisman affair. Prosecutor Alberto Nisman had recently filed a damning report alleging that both the Presidents Kirchner, Christine and her deceased husband whom she succeeded as President, along with their foreign minister and other officials conspired to cover up Iran's involvement in the 1994 bombing of a Jewish community center in Buenos Aires. But on the eve of his testimony before Congress, Nisman was found dead in his apartment from a gunshot wound to the temple. A gun and a shell casing were found near his body. The apartment was locked from the inside.

"Ah," the young man replies. "Did you not read the news today?"

"No, what happened?"

"All the charges against Kirchner were dropped. The judge found the case was totally flawed. Kirchner had no involvement with the Iranians. No evidence she colluded or received payment to cover up the bombing."

Time to introduce ourselves. She's Mandy; he's Marco. *Why does everybody in this country have a name that begins with M?* They're locals. Young. Maybe late twenties. Marco is an accountant; Mandy, a researcher. Attractive and engaging, they seem plugged in to what's happening. We are John and Nancy visiting from the States. We love Buenos Aires.

"So, what's your view?" I ask. "Sounds like you agree with today's decision." Mandy is quick to answer. "We do."

"And, I suppose the earth is the center of the universe and there is no such thing as global warming, evolution and gravity," I say.

"Ha. Don't misunderstand," Mandy says, "we are not ideologues; we are not Ks—supporters of de Kirchner are referred to as Ks—we are totally apolitical. But here, ethics comes in many shades of gray. Kirchner's opponents say she was paid off by the Iranians to cover up the bombing. K's supporters say she has no reason to take a bribe. She is already one of the wealthiest people in Argentina."

"Oh, and rich people never have people killed. Iran would never support a terrorist attack on Jews? And, have you heard, Putin is a pacifist?"

I'm expecting a laugh. Mandy frowns; Marco forces a smile. Maybe, I should cut the sarcasm.

Nancy asks, "What about the press? Doesn't the press get at the truth?"

Marco's retort comes at us as a well-practiced counterpunch. "What truth? What is truth? Who's to say? Each side has its own view. And, there are never just two sides. Not just Republican versus Democrat like in the USA. Here, our politics are more complicated. Multiple parties. Multiple factions. Whatever one side says, the press will dutifully quote exactly what is said. And, then they will ask the opinion of the opposition. Whatever the responses, the press will report accurately. In this way, the press feels it's doing its job. As I said, truth is in the eyes of the beholder."

Using a bit of Italian, I say, "My *verita* is not your *verita*."

Marco gets my drift. "Precisely, John. We all have different experiences, different backgrounds, therefore our truths, our *verite*, are different. Absolute truth is an abstraction. It is not reality." Then he adds, "At least not in Argentina."

Hmmmm. Another way Argentina is so Italian! Truth or *verita* is also a favorite subject with Italians. To them, truth is totally subjective, or relative. The last Pope, Gregory, railed against what he called the *dictatorship of relativism*. To him, some truths, like those found in the Ten Commandments or the Catholic bible, are absolute. I suppose, he also believed in the Pius IX doctrine that the Pope is infallible. Garibaldi was so dismayed by that concept that he named his favorite donkey *Pio Nono*, Pius IX. When asked about Gregory's absolutism, the current Pope, Francis, said he agreed, but then added, "everyone has his own idea of good and evil and must choose the good and fight the evils as he conceives them." Talk about doublespeak. Then again, Francis is an Argentine. Gregory is German. And, according to Garibaldi, Pius IX was an ass. As Harry Truman once said: "Where you stand on a subject, depends on where you sit."

"Marco, your politicians sound a lot like ours," I say. "According to Donald Trump, we're being invaded by Mexican immigrants. But, the fact is more people migrate to Mexico every year than the other way. And, what about China? Our politicians tell us China is destroying our economy. Yet, unemployment is at the lowest levels in decades, consumers have more money in their pockets, housing prices have rebounded, inflation is non-existent, the dollar is strong, gas prices are low, people are living longer, and our stock market is at record highs. I'm not saying our economy is not impacted by globalization, but—give me a break."

Marco seems to like my rant. He's laughing. "The problem," he says, "is cable news. Each of us gets to listen to the news we want. News that agrees with our opinions. Here in Buenos Aires, I can get twenty or thirty different news channels, including Sky, BBC, Fox and CNN."

"Each in our own silo," Nancy says.

"Yup." I say. "The Nazis did it with the People's Radio. Mass produced. So cheap, even the poorest homes in pre-war Germany had them. They could only receive German frequencies. No shortwave. No outside views. What the Nazis did for Germany, cable news allows us to do to ourselves. Talk about progress."

Matilda returns to our table. "I can tell, you're enjoying Clark's. How was everything? Would you like dessert? Coffee?"

I smile and say, "Nancy and I will each have Clark's famous Garibaldi cocktail. No dessert."

Marco, without missing a beat, says "Mandy will have coffee and the flan. No dessert for me but I will have a Coke, you know, *The Real Thing.*"

GETTING GAUCHO

May your stomach never grumble.
May your heart never ache.
May your horse never stumble
May your cinch never break.

COWBOY BLESSING

SAN ANTONIO DE ARECO, ARGENTINA

"Would you like a horse? Or would you rather take the wagon?"

I pause for a moment. It's been years since I was on a horse and the last experience wasn't a good one. I came away with a cracked coccyx and had to sit on a donut pillow for six months. *Oh, what the heck. It's only for an hour. How many chances will I have to ride a gaucho horse?* Besides, wagons are for children and old people, not me.

"I'll take the horse." I shoot John a questioning look, and he nods his agreement.

"I'll ride the horse too," he says. *My brave husband.*

We're finishing our tour of the house at El Ombu with the owner, Eva Boelcke. The *estancia*, or ranch, is near San Antonio de Arceo in the pampas area northwest of Buenos Aires. Our drive here took something over an hour and we're to spend the day. Like many American dude ranches, the *estancias* offer

71

overnight accommodations and meals. This one is part farm, part ranch and part B & B. The late-colonial style mansion, built in 1880, isn't large, its single story crowned by a broad decorative border and capped by what appears to be a balcony. Underneath, a wide porch wraps around the stuccoed building. The interior, white stucco with thick, dark wood trim, has tall windows that let the breezes in. Long wooden tables in this dining room must make communal meals especially enjoyable. I notice two framed items on a brick column, a photo and a newspaper clipping, and ask the owner who it is.

"That's Pereira, one of our gauchos. He's a famous horse tamer, well known in the country. His father was famous as well, and taught his secrets to his son."

The age of the man in the article's photo could be thirty-five or fifty. Slight and wiry with a thick, drooping mustache, his red cap nearly covers his eyes. In the black-and-white photo that hangs above it, he's much older, looking wistfully to the left of the lens, his hair graying, cheekbones jutting from his thin face. Eyes, brows, mustache and even his hat droop in sadness or solitude.

"Come outside now, and I'll show you where we'll have our lunch," says Eva. She points to the tables clustered under a giant tree, one for each group that's come today.

"What kind of tree is that?" I ask. It looks as though it could be a clump of trees, except a bark-covered mound sits in the center.

"That's the ombu, the tree that gives its name to our *estancia*. Actually, it isn't a tree at all. It's a bush. But this one is over a hundred years old. The ombu is the national tree of Argentina. Uruguay too. They're the only 'tree' that can survive in the pampas because they need very little water."

Ombu. The word reminds me of *ombra*, the Italian word for shade. This ombu certainly provides some *ombra* today.

"Have a walk around," Eva says. "We'll call you to the horses in a little while."

We stroll around the side of the building, admiring the thick ivy that covers the porch's pillars and climbs over the balcony. Tall trees near the house provide plenty of shade and ornamental plants line the walkway leading to a now only-decorative well. Around the rear of the building we come upon the outdoor kitchen, an open shed where a five-foot grill is piled with various meats over charcoal ashes. The aroma of smoky flesh teases our nostrils. I nod to the aproned chef who grins and rattles some Spanish, gesturing to his grill. Moments later the call comes and we head for the corral.

About fifteen of us will be riding and we're each helped onto the thick sheepskin that covers the saddle. Gauchos live on a horse so their saddles are designed for comfort. *This* is how a saddle should feel. It's like sitting on a pillow-top mattress. I watched as a couple of the horses were readied. First a blanket to protect the horse. Then the small saddle, but not a hard leather one like we use in America. These are almost flat, about four inches thick and made of three layers, all padded, the top one soft suede. Once it's secured to the horse, the four-inch thick sheepskin is strapped over it. Atop my chestnut mare I look over at my husband gathering his reins. Red Phillies cap on his head, Chinese symbol on his black t-shirt, he doesn't look much like a gaucho. I guess I don't either—red floral t-shirt, black visor, and cotton pants. The soft web band of my little purse crosses my chest like an ammunition belt. *Wonder what Garibaldi would think of us?*

Like us, riding wasn't native to him. His wife, Anita, taught him. Her father raised his daughter like a boy, so she learned to ride early in life.

The gauchos were usually *mestizos*, people of mixed European and Indian heritage, but they could also be white, black or mulatto. They were excellent riders who could break a wild horse in a day and used a whip and a *bola* to herd the animals. The *bola* consists of three long cords of braided leather tied together with a knot at one end. On the opposite ends, each is tied with a stone about the size of a tangerine. To bring down an animal, the gaucho holds the knotted end and whirls the braided cords over his head, then aims for the animal. When released, the cords separate in the air and wrap around the legs of the animal, causing it to falter or fall so the thrower can catch it. Gauchos were tough men, strong men, and amazing horsemen. Riding quickly, cutting in and out of a herd while hurling a *bola*, or cracking a whip, the gaucho was a formidable athlete.

They could also fight when necessary. A typical costume was a woolen poncho, scarf knotted around the neck, loose pants tucked into their boots, and a wide leather belt with a long dagger called a *facón* tucked in at the back. Garibaldi not only learned their horse and *bola* moves, he adopted much of their costume for the balance of his life. Photos, paintings, and statues show him wearing the knotted scarf at his neck, and often a poncho-like cloak. Like the gauchos, he was adaptable to the changing climate, the landscape of prairie-like grass. A hard way of life was nothing new to him.

He must have been a natural athlete, one of those men whose body molds itself effortlessly for whatever purpose he chooses. When he came to South America he'd already morphed from swimmer to seaman, to captain. Mastering the art of horsemanship and a new weapon wouldn't have been difficult.

Our own ride is quite easy. A gentle walk and occasional trot through the high grassland where the only sound is the swishing of the grasses and the horses' snorts. Leading our group is the man I'd seen in the photos. He looks even older now, a little grayer, a dark blue scarf tied neatly round the neck of his light blue shirt. We make a long loop and return to the corral where I give my mare a few grateful pats. The smell of her horsey flesh clings to my hands, an odor I like, but decide to wash before our lunch. *I'm not a bit uncomfortable.* I could have stayed in that saddle all day.

Our little group from the city—a Vietnamese couple from Ontario with their two youngsters and a couple from Scotland—gathers at a round table. This will be a typical *asado*, the traditional meat-laden meal of Argentina. The old-time gauchos lived nearly exclusively on meat and our lunch would make them proud, all of it coming from this ranch. The first course is a plate piled with several different grilled selections. A crispy one, we are told, is intestines. *Very good.* Others are sausages and marinated pork. Several salads come next and then the main meat course, ribs and several cuts of smoky steak. It all takes over an hour. Delicious, fleshy overload.

With coffee, the entertainment begins. The old gaucho from the photo appears with a guitar, pulls up a chair and plants the instrument across his lap. He's a fine musician and the instrument resonates with deep tones like an old wine. He sings. I'm not sure the subject, but it sounds like a lonely story, a cowboy equivalent of the melancholy tango. When the music stops the horse show starts. A muscular young man and a beautiful brown-and-white paint horse ride over.

Eva explains. "This is a demonstration of the gaucho 'horse whisperer.' The horse is completely in the hands of the gaucho. Whatever the man wants, the horse will allow."

As she speaks, he dismounts and begins stroking, caressing the horse's side. Moving to the rear, he gently rubs each rear leg then repositions them farther apart. Crawling between them and under the animal's belly he emerges in the front. Always stroking, stroking, he lifts a front leg, kneels and gently places it on his knee. Completely relaxed, the horse allows all the movements of its legs—out, back, curved, straightened. The man mounts, trots a circle around the yard and returns. Constantly caressing the horse, he leans forward, rises, and plants his knees on the horse's left side at the front and rear of the saddle. Pulling backward on the right rein, he backs the animal into a crouch and then down on its side. He strokes its back, rear, neck, lays across it and strokes the stomach, legs and face. Gently, he turns the animal onto its back, legs in the air. He sits on its stomach reaching forward to caress the neck and face. Extending the front legs he places them on his shoulders. He dismounts. Gently again, he rolls the horse back onto its side and allows it to get up. Mounting, he stands on his saddle, hands extended in the air. Applause.

Once again, he backs the horse into a crouch and down onto its side. He walks around, lies on the grass, his body curved into the horse's chest, face on the animal's cheek. They're still for a full minute.

"Who would like to do the same?" Eva asks.

Is she kidding? Of course I will. John snaps a photo. Me curled up with the beautiful horse, my hand on its nose. Handsome gaucho sitting at the base of its neck, smiling. What could be more memorable?

Gaucho and horse. A merging of man and beast. Garibaldi had such a horse, Marsala. A white stallion, the one the Hero rides in all the paintings. In Caprera we saw where the stallion is buried, under a marble plaque at the corner of the great barn.

Garibaldi took more than horsemanship from this area. He took the gauchos. They became his Red Shirts. Fierce fighters, they followed him to Italy with weapons unseen by European troops. He took Andres Agular, a freed slave and battle companion who was with Garibaldi until his own death in Rome. And he took a wife. One who taught him her native gaucho skills then rode into battle alongside him. It's hard for me to imagine that kind of woman. But I can imagine the kind of man Garibaldi was. Rugged and charismatic. One who moved with the grace of Baryshnikov and strength of the Babe. Who with escape skills of MacGiver eluded captors and captivated women. Who loved to sit at night with a guitar and sing or dance. One who could inspire students and artists and cowboys to fight for freedom. Who wouldn't fall for that kind of man?

IMPROVISING IN MONTEVIDEO

I don't believe people are looking for the meaning of life as much as they are looking for the experience of being alive.

JOSEPH CAMPBELL

MONTEVIDEO, URUGUAY

"That's it! Across the street. 314. That is definitely number 314. And, this is *Via 25 De Mayo*. So, that's got to be it. That's his house."

I'm excited. We've come a long way to see it. Garibaldi's House. He and Anita lived in the rear of this little town house with their four children from 1844 to 1847 when he led the Italian Legion. His exploits made him a folk hero around the world.

I can't wait to look inside. We cross the street, stand in front of a two story gray stucco row house with a heavy, faded-green, double door at street level. The Plexiglas sign to the right of the door holds an official-looking letter-size document that says in Spanish:

Casa de José Garibaldi: This house was the residence of Giuseppe Garibaldi and his family during the Uruguayan Civil War. In key battles against secessionist forces and their Argentine allies, Garibaldi distinguished himself by leading Unionist forces to

77

victories on both land and sea. The house is open Monday through Friday from 11:00 to 16:45 hours and contains a permanent exposition of paintings, photos and historical elements recalling the life of the heroic Italian.

The door is locked. I knock. No answer. Knock harder. No answer. The window to the right of the sign is locked and shuttered from the inside. I tap on the glass with my keys. Nobody home. Nancy takes my picture next to the sign. She'll post it later on Facebook. All our followers will know we've found the Garibaldi house. But why is it not open? Today is Thursday. Could it be some sort of holiday?

A man in a dark business suit is walking by carrying a thermos bottle and a briefcase. I point to the sign. Ask with my hands, *hat gives?* He shrugs his shoulders, looks at me as if to say, I have no clue; he walks on. I repeat the pantomime with a well-dressed woman and then again with an overly-muscular female jogger. More shrugs.

Directly across the street I notice a tall, thin, middle-aged man peering out from the window of a shop that features wooden crafts. He's waving at me. I wave back. Good. Someone who knows what's going on. I ask Nancy to stand guard at the green door while I bop across the street to the craft shop.

"Do you speak English?" He doesn't. I try my version of Spanish. *"Casa di Garibaldi. Est abierta?"* Is it open? He shakes his head and says something that sounds like *chiuda permanente.* Closed Permanently? *Si, si,* permanently closed. Waving his hands in front of his leather apron, he makes like a baseball umpire calling a runner safe. But, I get the message. We are not safe. We are out. Out of luck. Locked out. The Garibaldi house is closed—permanently.

This can't be. What does this guy know? He carves wooden figures. He's just a neighbor, not an official. Nonetheless, I thank him for his help, pet his sleepy dog and leave.

As I jog back across the street toward her, Nancy can read the umpire's call on my face. I spell it out. "He says the place is closed—permanently."

"Permanently? No way!" she almost shouts. "We've come five thousand miles to see the Garibaldi House, and it's closed? Permanently? Look, the website doesn't say it's closed." Pointing to her i-Phone, she adds "According to their website, it's open every weekday from 11 a.m to 4:45 p.m. It's 11:45."

Of course I know what the website says. We checked it last night. Used Google Translate. It says exactly what the sign says. Neither says anything about the house being closed.

What to do?

Nancy is already on it. Googling. "Seems like there are several Montevideo museums that fall under the general umbrella of Cultura. There's a wine museum. A Gaucho and Money Museum. A Fine Arts museum. The nearest one, the Museum of the Visual Arts, is one block up and two blocks over."

"Really? A Gaucho and Money Museum? Combined?"

"Yes," she says. "That's what it's called. The Gaucho and Money Museum. No kidding."

"Wow. Who curates something like that? John Wayne? Zorro? The Cisco Kid? Certainly not Garibaldi. He and Anita may have been gauchos, but together they could barely earn enough to feed their kids."

Nancy's brow furrows. "Wasn't it Anita who got him the great deal on surplus red shirts?"

"Yup. Lucky thing, too. If she had gotten him the gross of brown pants he wanted, we might now be referring to his legionnaires as the Hosensheitzers, the shit pants."

She laughs. "I think we should go to the Museum of Visual Arts—see what we can learn."

As we walk toward the museum, I blurt out: "Admiral Brown."

"What about Admiral Brown?" Nancy is looking at me to see if my mind had spilled out onto the sidewalk.

"Admiral Brown," I say again. "Brown was his nemesis. Anita may have taught Garibaldi to ride a horse, but it was Argentina's Admiral Brown who destroyed Garibaldi's fleet. Forced him to flee overland. Forced him to switch from sailor to soldier."

"OK. But why are you fixating on Brown at this moment?"

"Why. I'll tell you why. Brown was in that house. Garibaldi's fiercest enemy. He visited the house. The goddamn house we can't get into. Damn it! If Brown could get in. Why can't we?"

Who was Admiral William Brown? Born 1777 in Ireland and raised in Philadelphia, Brown was Garibaldi's senior by thirty years. Yet the two combatants had eerily parallel careers. Orphaned at age ten, Brown escaped the mean streets of Philadelphia to become a cabin boy aboard a merchant ship. He was a quick learner, well on his way to becoming a captain. But before he was twenty his ship was boarded by a British Man-O-War and he was taken captive, forced to serve for five years as a British seaman. During the Napoleonic Wars, his ship was sunk by the French. Brown, an expert swimmer like Garibaldi, swam two miles to shore where he was captured by French authorities and imprisoned at Metz. From that point on, Brown's story reads like a variation on a theme by Garibaldi. Brown escapes from Metz. He's recaptured, sent to Verdun. Again, he escapes; this time to Germany. Eventually he gets to England where he obtains work as a merchant seaman at Chitty Shipping. In 1809 he marries the boss's daughter, Elizabeth Chitty. The newlyweds decide to combine business with pleasure by delivering cargo to Montevideo and Buenos Aires where they establish a shipping venture along the De la Plata.

Like Garibaldi, Brown's civilian life is interrupted by short violent spurts of war. In 1810, both Argentina and Uruguay were seeking independence from Spain. When Spanish war ships destroyed one of his merchant ships, Brown accepted a commission from Argentina, where he would attain the rank of Admiral and eventually be recognized as the Father of the Navy.

"Admiral Brown," Nancy says. "We have a bunch of pictures of his green tomb at the Recoleta Cemetery in Buenos Aires."

"Yes," I say. "Except for maybe Eva Peron, I'd bet Brown is the most popular figure buried there."

"What about here?" Nancy asks. "How do the Uruguayans view him?"

"You know, despite the devastating blockade of Montevideo, Brown is still revered in Uruguay because when he destroyed the much larger Spanish fleet in 1814, it led to independence from Spain for Uruguay as well as Argentina. The blockade came thirty years later during the messy Uruguayan Civil War;

Argentina was aligned with the breakaway Oribe/Rivera faction. Garibaldi favored Rosas and the Union."

"Odd. Brown and Garibaldi were outsiders who ultimately became more famous than their respective leaders," Nancy says.

Despite their heroic achievements, both men had to contend with jealousy and back biting. Both were imprisoned for insubordination. More than once. Argentina threw Brown in prison after the War of Independence and again after the Brazilian War. The last time was for three years. Three years! Imagine! This great hero. Liberator. Father of the Navy. Jailed for three years. The Argentines released him the first time because they were getting their asses kicked in the war with Brazil. They needed Brown to bail them out. And, he did.

Here's what it says in Wikipedia. *On June 11, 1827 at Los Pozos eleven Argentine ships under the command of Admiral William Brown routed thirty-one Brazilian warships and led to the peace Treaty of Montevideo signed on October 4, 1827.* But when Brown pursued Brazilian war ships into the Pacific Ocean, he went too far. That's when he landed in jail for three years. Insubordinate foreigner, they called him.

"So how did Brown and Garibaldi become adversaries?" Nancy asks.

"Similar story. With Brown sitting in jail, Garibaldi was making Argentina's navy look silly. So, her leaders once again went hat in hand to Brown. And, once again, Brown did what Brown always did. He rose to the occasion. In command of four schooners, three brigs, and five smaller vessels he chased Garibaldi and his three converted merchant ships all over the Rio de La Plata and finally onto the shoals of the river Parana. From five hundred meters out, Brown's ships pounded Garibaldi with cannon fire."

In his *Memoirs*, Garibaldi describes his predicament:

Our ships were reduced to hulks. The corvette, in spite of attempts to plug the leaks, was taking water so fast that it was difficult to keep it afloat even by pumping continuously and using everyone to take a turn...There were many dead and even more wounded. The remaining crew, although completely exhausted, could not rest because of excess water in the hold. Yet, there was still gunpowder and there was still shot, and so we had to fight, not to win and not to save ourselves, but to keep our honor.

"Brown's action caused Garibaldi to burn his own ships and escape over land. By the time he got back to Montevideo, Brown's ships had the city under siege."

"So, that's when Garibaldi formed the Italian Legion, the famous Red-Shirts?"

"Yes," I say.

With Montevideo under siege by Brown's fleet, there was no money to buy uniforms for his recruits. So, he and Anita outfitted them with surplus red shirts used by slaughterhouse workers. When he led a few hundred of his Red-Shirts to a stunning victory over a much larger combined Rebel and Argentine force at the town of San Antonio do Salto, Garibaldi and his Red Shirts became famous.

After San Antonio do Salto, his regiment swelled with new recruits. Although officially called the Italian Legion, truth is it was comprised of a polyglot of European exiles, misfits, and freed slaves. It was these Red Shirts who would become the nucleus of the force returning to Italy in 1848 to fight for unification. But not before Garibaldi had one more shot at Brown and the Argentine Navy. On August 21, 1844 he carried out a surprise attack near Bucco and captured an Argentine brig and schooner filled with precious flour, sugar and other goods sorely needed in Montevideo. Once in port, Brown's fleet blocked his escape. Though by then the goods were unloaded and distributed. Six days later, Garibaldi pulled a similar stunt by commandeering a "friendly" Spanish ship loaded with supplies. On September 18th, he used the two captured vessels to attack two of Brown's warships causing their retreat. The besieged population, which had watched the daytime encounter from the roof-tops cheered his name. *Garibaldi. Garibaldi. Viva Garibaldi.* But during the blockade, Anita and the four children endured terrible hardships. In December 1845, their daughter, Rosita, succumbed to influenza.

Before Garibaldi left for Italy, a retired Admiral Brown visited his home to pay respects. There, Brown would famously tell Garibaldi how much he regretted not having had the pleasure of capturing the general years earlier. Had he done so, Brown said, he would not have had to wait so long to tell Garibaldi how much he admired him. Twenty years later, one of Garibaldi's grandsons would be given the name William, a tribute to this old adversary.

In a few minutes we're in front of an imposing three story mansion that is the Museum of Visual Arts. Just inside to the left is an information counter. The uniformed young man sitting there tells us without our asking "*Libero.*" Free. Admission is free.

I follow my perfunctory "*Gracias*" with an interrogation.

No, he does not speak English or Italian. Nonetheless, I proceed in Italian. We manage.

Yes, he knows the Garibaldi house.

Yes, he knows it's closed.

Yes, Permanently.

He tells me why: No *Dirección*.

Uruguay has a new president. Until he makes appointments, we have no *Dirección*. Direction. Meanwhile, I come to work. I do my job. I get paid. No *Dirección*.

Yes, there is a curator.

Senora Sanchez.

Do you wish to speak with her?

Si. Si.

He picks up the phone, punches in a few numbers, speaks to someone in hushed Spanish. Hands me the phone.

The voice on the other end of the line is warm and friendly.

"Hello. This is Senora Sanchez."

Finally. Someone who speaks English.

"Good morning. We are authors, John and Nancy Petralia, from the United States. For our new book, *Looking for Garibaldi*, we're writing about the places Garibaldi lived and fought. We'd like to see his home. We've come five thousand miles. Can you help us get in?"

"They've closed the house for budget reasons. It's closed to visitors until further notice."

"I understand. But, can someone get us in? We just want to take a few photos. Get the feel of the place. We'd be so grateful."

"It's not possible."

"All we need is for someone to open the door. If there are no lights, I'll bring a flashlight. From the website, we already know there's not much to see. But there's no substitute for experiencing the place in the flesh. For us, it's important to get a sense of how he, Anita and four children coped during the siege. I want to see how they lived; I know they only had two rooms, not the whole house. I want to touch the walls they touched. I want to walk the floors they walked. I want to see what Admiral Brown saw when he came to visit. Senora Sanchez, I need to get into that house."

"Signore Petralia. How long will you be in Montevideo?"

"We leave on Tuesday."

"Where are you staying?"

"Our apartment is on via Colon, in the old port."

"Mr. Petralia, we close today at 4:00 p.m. Tomorrow, Friday, we have a staff meetings. None of us is available over the weekend. But, if you return on Monday at 10:00 a.m., I'll arrange to have someone go with you to the Garibaldi House."

"Oh, thank you. Thank you. Thank you, so much."

Going to Punta del Este for the weekend seemed a good idea at the time. Our Montevideo apartment had lost its charm. Street noises. Non-functioning microwave. Lousy air conditioning. Neighbors who partied all night. We needed some fresh air, sunshine, sea and sand. So, we rented a car and drove about fifty miles to Uruguay's version of Rio. Because we were to be there for only two nights, we splurged on five stars at the beach right next to the site of a new Trump Tower. Very luxurious. Despite a weekend of rain, the decision to go seemed right—at the time.

Once at the hotel, the incessant rain could not dim our spirits. Indeed, the hotel's indoor spa and hot spring pool became our hangout for most of Saturday. Save for some very attentive servers, we were the only two people at the pool. On Saturday night, we drove into town to what the concierge claimed to be the best restaurant in the region.

No, I don't know if the source of our problem was the restaurant, snacks and drinks at poolside, the pool, or brushing our teeth with tap water. But, by the time we returned to Montevideo on Sunday night, I had it.

Diarrhea. Despite taking loads of Kaopectate, I'm miserable. Every time I think the medicine is working, I'm proved wrong—spending more time in the bathroom than in bed. Nancy had a mild case; this morning, she's feeling much better. I'm not. And, today is Monday. This is the day we're going to Garibaldi's house. We're supposed to meet Senora Sanchez at the Museum of Visual Arts at 10:00 a.m. From there someone will take us to the Garibaldi House; let us in. But, I am really scared. I can't seem to last more than an hour at a clip before having to run to a bathroom. This morning, I would have run out for Depends but the stores don't open until 10:00 a.m. Instead, I have a half dozen paper towels shoved in my underwear and I pray. The museum is only ten minutes away. I have not eaten anything for more than twenty-four hours. Nothing in my stomach, I can make it. From the Museum to Garibaldi's house is another ten minutes. I can do this.

What's this? The sign on the Museum of Visual Arts says closed. Closed on Monday. "No way," I scream. Senora Sanchez told us to meet her here today.

Nancy knocks. A guard answers. In Spanish he says, "We're closed."

That's when I say, "Signora Sanchez."

He looks at us and pauses. "*Si, si.* Enter."

Once inside, I ask him if there is a *bagno*, a bathroom. He points the way. I make it to the bathroom just in time. That was close.

When I return to the front desk, two women are there speaking with Nancy. I learn neither is Señora Sanchez. Instead, she has selected these two to escort us. The taller, slimmer, younger of the two is Mariana, an art historian. The shorter, stouter woman is Carina; she has worked at the Garibaldi house as a guide. Both women will accompany us. We're dignitaries on our way to a private tour. Wow!

For me, the walk over to the Garibaldi house takes place on a high wire. No net. What if the urge hits me. About half way there, I ask Clara if the house has a bathroom. "*Si, si,*" she says.

Once in, I ask her to point the way. She does. I run in. Relief.

Oh no. The water is turned off. I can't flush. I try the sink. Same thing. No water. I look for a valve under the toilet. There is a valve. I turn it. No water. There must be a main valve. But, where? As I look around, I can hear the ladies giving Nancy the tour.

Ginger ale. God bless me. A nearly full twelve-ounce bottle of ginger ale is sitting on the window sill directly over the toilet. I take it down, pour the contents into the toilet. "Please, please let it flush." It does.

No toilet paper. To clean up, I use two of the paper towels stuffed in my underwear. When I rejoin Nancy and the two guides, I say, "Thank you for the tour. Very informative. I have to leave."

Nancy looks at me, understands: "I am so sorry. My husband is not well." She shakes hands with the two ladies, and repeats, "My husband is ill."

I do not extend my hand. We leave.

On our way back to our apartment, I spot a trash can. I reach into my pocket, remove two carefully wrapped paper towels, deposit them, and think to myself: "hosensheitzer."

RETURNING HOME

Every man, every woman, carries in heart and mind the image of the ideal place, the right place the one true home, known or unknown, actual or visionary.

EDWARD ABBEY

MILAN, ITALY

Outside my window, three thousand feet below, Italy is a crazy-quilt of green. Traditional red tile covers the roofs of the occasional village or town. Only industrial buildings appear different. I can easily pick out the ancient towns, streets wriggling out from the central piazza or church tower like a mountain stream, growing wider as they go, but never tamed. Newer villages have the gridded look you find in America, but they're more compact. Even Milan is wound tight around its haphazard center, its only exception the expanding ring roads that mark the fortress walls and modern circular highways. Watching our slow descent I'm surprised to feel my eyes tear up. The place of my heart has pulled me tight again.

I wonder if this is how Garibaldi felt returning to Italy from South America in 1848? He must have been homesick for his beloved homeland after his thirteen-year exile. It's been nearly five years since we lived in Italy and every return is filled with anticipation.

A few hours later, our baggage tucked into the Novotel in Cardano Al Campo, we're stretching our legs with a meander into the tiny village. There's not much

87

here. Not even a real *piazza*. Just a church with a wide front terrace where some sort of political event is happening with tents, and brochures, and townsfolk engaged in lively discussion. Around the corner we find a bar with outdoor seating and choose a table under the portico. The *barista* appears immediately.

"*Due spritz*," John says. Our favorite Italian *apertivo* is made with Aperol and prosecco and served throughout the country.

"*Due caffè*," she says in a flat voice.

"*No, no. SPRITZ. Con Aperol.*"

She raises her eyebrows. "*Oh, SPREETZ*," she says and turns to go inside.

Pronunciation. It trips us up again. You've got to say it just right, or the Italians don't understand. So we laugh, trying to reset our ears and tongues to this marvelous, mysterious, language we mangle so well.

A few little shops are tucked under the portico which surrounds a parking lot. Next door, intertwining cultures in a way many Italians abhor, the pizza place also serves kabobs. Above, on the second floor are curvy iron balconies, one covered in purple-and-white flowers where a boy of about two is jumping with excitement as he calls "*Papa, Papa*" to a man exiting his car below. Our *SPREETZ* arrives accompanied by olives, crispy breadsticks, and tiny sandwiches topped by a slice of cherry tomato and a toothpick. The pick's protective paper is artfully crunched into a miniature flag. It's a detail that shows the Italians' sense of style I love so much.

"Let's ask her," I say to John when we step inside later to pay.

"*C'è una Via Garibaldi qui?*"

"*Sì*," she answers and directs us to a street a few blocks away. We're off again on our exploration game—looking for Garibaldi—the way we navigate each new town and village searching for the place that honors him. The route is through a residential neighborhood of modern Italian homes. Two- and three-story rectangular stucco boxes painted white, yellow, and tan, their dark brown shutters are closed tight and flowers trail from some of the balconies. At a corner we find it: Via Garibaldi. Not a grand avenue but an average street lined with homes and stores. We can't find any plaque commemorating the Hero of Two Worlds. But like every Italian town we've visited there's *something*: this simple road is tribute to the Unifier of Italy.

"It's a little village," I say to John who looks disappointed. "Guess you can't expect too much. They don't even have a real central *piazza*. We know we'll find him in Bologna a few days from now."

BOLOGNA, ITALY

"Giuliano, c'e un museo della citta. Non era aperto l'ultima volta che siamo stati qui." There's a museum about the city. It wasn't open last time we were here. We're on our way from the airport back to our friends' apartment where we'll stay for a couple days. "Can we go while we're in Bologna?"

I can tell by his tone Giuliano is pleased. *"Certo, Nancy."* Sure. Beside me in the back seat, Teresa adds her agreement.

I work out the Italian words in my head and say, "I read a lot about it online. I remember you telling us when it opened—and how much you liked it. It seems to have some excellent exhibits." I hope he'll be pleased I've looked into Bologna's newest attraction. Like every Italian, Giuliano is extremely proud and protective of his city. He and Teresa were upset five years ago when we decided to leave Bologna and move to Parma.

From the driver's seat Giuliano says over his shoulder, "It's a very good museum."

I remember when it opened. He emailed us articles announcing the occasion. John translated some of them for us. It wasn't like what you'd read in the States—what, when, where, why, how. The Italians write differently. They circle around a topic with flowery wording often only obliquely related to the point. More interesting to me than the text were the photos which featured the creative design of the building interior and exhibits.

Teresa leans toward me. "After dinner tonight we can go. And tomorrow you will meet Louisa." I can hear the delight in her voice at the mention of Louisa's name. We've heard about Louisa for nearly five years, the woman our friends visit every year when they come to America.

This get-together is a happy coincidence. Louisa, who lives in Chicago, works for a pharmaceutical company and travels to Europe with some frequency. She has a meeting in Rome, but she's coming a day early so she can spend time in Bologna with her dear friends the Vitalis. Louisa is their "adopted" American daughter. When we were living in Italy, I remember Teresa telling me about the birth of Louisa's twins— as excited as if they were her own grandchildren. A couple years ago while we were visiting with them in Bologna, we went one evening with our friends to buy a double stroller because Louisa was bringing her daughters over to visit.

At the apartment building they own, we muscle our bags up the wide, granite stairs. On the landing, mid-point on each floor, I take a moment to glance out the window and take a deep breath. I'm more than relieved when Teresa stops at the third floor and wraps on the door. Their daughter Christina opens it. *"Benvenuto,"* she says giving all of us a traditional *baci* on each cheek. "Welcome. How was your trip over?"

"Bene, bene," we both say. Good.

"Oh, here's Alessandro," Christina says, as her younger son steps into the doorway. I hardly recognize the tall young man, his looks morphing from childish to dreamy. He greets us with a *ciao* and the two-cheek kiss. Last time we saw him he was just fourteen and too shy to have done so. He was planning to go to cooking school at the time. *I wonder how he's made out.* Before we return to the stairs, Christina confirms the planned family dinner for the next evening.

"We'll see you tomorrow," Teresa says and resumes her climb up the next flight. John and I re-shoulder our backpacks with a sigh. Giuliano grabs my carry-on and I brace for the next two-story ascent.

When we've settled ourselves in their bedroom, Teresa appears at the doorway. "You two take a rest. We'll have dinner in a while." *I'm not tired, I just got a bit winded from the stair climb.*

"No, I'll help," I insist and follow her to the kitchen. John and Giuliano go to hover over the computer and catch up on emails, their rapid Italian chatter beyond my comprehension.

"Alessandro's so grown-up," I say as I chop the salad veggies. "How are his studies at the restaurant school coming?"

"He's enjoying it. Now he's working in a local restaurant. That's part of the curriculum."

"I remember. All the students have work-study programs. It's a good system."

Teresa pulls her homemade pasta from the freezer and sautés fresh radicchio to toss with it. Later, at the kitchen table, Giuliano pours the water and local wine. For dessert, Teresa's biscotti and fruit. Simple food—the essence of the Italian table. After the meal we're off for the museum.

As we walk down Via Indipendenza, the portico seems cleaner than I remember and I mention this to our friends. "Yes," says Giuliano. "There's been a new emphasis on cleaning up the graffiti, especially in the most visible places." Graffitied walls and pillars along the ancient porticos had disturbed us when we lived here. We couldn't understand why people would deface such beauty. It seemed a city where no one cared. *I wonder if this new, cleaner city would have made a different first impression on me.*

Along the granite-paved sidewalks of the porticos I'm enjoying my reacquaintance with familiar stores—shoes, household goods, cell phones, stores with skimpy, youthful clothing, and artful fashions for the more mature. Sidewalk tables are crowded for *appertivo*—the early evening time for drinks and snacks—and echoes of lively conversations reverberate through the arched porticos. At the corner of Piazza del 8 Agosto, the intersecting street widens where it leads to the market square to our left. Enterprising crafters have set up their tables across the barricaded entrance offering leather goods, clothing and beaded jewelry. In the next block, a thicket of trees, clustered like green pompoms of a cheerleader line, obscures the hotels and restaurants on our left. Midway down that block, emerging from those treetop pompoms like the quarterback taking the field, Garibaldi sits astride his horse, still keeping watch on the passersby from his granite pedestal.

No one takes any notice.

His relaxed, pensive pose sets me wondering what he could be thinking. Aside from motorized traffic, the city must look much the same as during his time. *More students for sure and probably more restaurants. Although you never fought here, Giuseppe, you must have been pleased by what happened after unification.* Napoleon had taken Bologna in 1789, but after his overthrow in 1815 it was returned to the Papal States. Two unsuccessful uprisings drove the occupying Austrian troops out temporarily before Garibaldi's Second War of Independence brought about the unification. In March of 1860, after Garibaldi's victories, the city voted to be annexed by the Kingdom of Sardinia, soon to be the Kingdom of Italy.

During World War II Bologna was a stronghold of the resistance movement. *Garibaldi would have liked that.* Then, after the war, it became the seat of the Italian Communist Party and remains so today. *Rule by the people—I think he would have approved of that too.* Garibaldi worked to turn his rocky terrain on Caprera into farmed land and built a lovely house for his family. But Bologna's laissez-faire Communist leadership hasn't even kept the ancient city clean. *I think Giuseppe would be disgusted. Maybe the new mayor will change things.*

"Oh, wow. Look at the *duomo*," I say as we cross Piazza Maggiore. "What a difference cleaning made." The lower part, the only part of the facade finished before funds ran out, has emerged from the grime, its white marble accentuated with blocks of pink. What a pity it was never completed. It *could* have rivaled the Vatican.

John grabs my hand to hurry me toward the museum. Beyond Piazza Maggiore the nearby streets are bustling. "I think it's much more lively than when we were here," he says.

"It's Friday evening. Perfect weather too, but I agree. Even with the economic crisis there's no shortage of patrons in the restaurants."

"It feels much more alive, more welcoming." He's right. Tonight I love being in Bologna. Five years—nearly two spent in Italy—have given me a new way of seeing this country.

From the street, Palazzo Pepoli, which houses the museum, is undistinguished except for a long banner which hangs beside its arched entrance. Inside, beneath a giant map of the city, we buy our tickets and learn we're just in time for a guided tour. Unfortunately for me, it's only in Italian. *Oh well.*

Our guide is an attractive young woman wearing a black-and-white-striped dress, her hair piled on her head. While she chatters in the first room, I wander around looking at all the maps, each one showing a different time in the development of the city. It's easier for me to try to puzzle out the wording on the signs than to follow the narration. I don't need her story to explain the exhibit in another room. I recognize it as the canopy that covers the icon of the Madonna from San Luca. When we lived here, we watched the procession of church officials, dignitaries, and everyday citizens follow her from the Saragozza Gate and along the street that fronted our apartment during the annual parade. Standing here now, I remember how the air was filled with their singing voices as they passed by us.

From behind a display at the corner of the room an irritated female voice interrupts our guide, who looks surprised. It belongs to a voluptuous "house-maid" who's dusting around the room. Dressed in white, 18th century flounce, a frilly cap covers her head. I don't need to understand the words to get her message. Scolding, waving her feather duster, she's telling us about life in her time, and the role of the saucy servant. As we move through the rooms she reappears frequently, even once crawling from under an exhibit, to interrupt our guide. Their banter is fun to watch even if I have no idea what they're talking about most of the time. "What did she say?" I ask John over and over. At the tour's end the two of them leave us in a room rimmed by busts of Bologna women who shaped the city's culture from the 13th to 17th century.

On our own we continue to explore and as usual I fall behind John and our friends. Museum details suck me in like a kid pulling mom toward the gelato stand. When I turn around in the hall of paintings, I'm alone. I catch up with everyone under water, at least it feels that way. The exhibit, in a long dark room, uses moving light to imitate the watery canals that once flowed through the city and now lie underground. The effect is mesmerizing and I'd like to stay here for a while, but everyone else has disappeared and I reluctantly follow.

One of Bologna's several nicknames is "The Learned," and there's an area that celebrates its contributions to literature, music, art and science. That's where we find the Marconi exhibit. Giuliano and Teresa took us to his home, just outside the city, a couple years ago. A tinkerer, not a trained scientist, Marconi simply intuited that radio waves could extend over the horizon. We stood in the second-floor window where he proved it. On the first floor of the home, I photographed

John holding a cordless phone about the size of a Shaquille O'Neal shoebox. Marconi intuited cell service too and reminded me of Steve Jobs in his prescience for the things we've never thought of that we can't live without.

Of course, John and I look for a Garibaldi exhibit. The single reference to him is a photo of his statue. The annotation says, "On July 8, 1900 the statue of the Hero of Two Worlds replaced that of Ugo Bassi which was moved to the barracks at San Gervassio." A hero in his own right, and chaplain of Garibaldi's army, Bassi was captured during the escape to San Marino, returned to the Austrians in Bologna, and executed. The street that meets Via Indipendenza near the Neptune fountain is named for him. His picture and story are on the panel next the Garibaldi photo. Next to that is a long description of the day King Vittorio Emmanuel II visited the city after the unification which, without Garibaldi, would probably not have happened. *I guess they assume everyone knows all about the Hero. And, it's a museum about Bologna. Still...*

When it's time to leave I'm the last one out. Despite being unable to understand three-quarters of what I tried to read, I wish I had more time. This museum celebrates a *city*—an unusual idea. In America we have the Museum of the City of New York and the Chicago History Museum, but I don't know of any other cities in the States with a museum dedicated to themselves. There's no Los Angeles one. Nor even one for the District of Columbia. In Philly we celebrate the birth of our nation at Independence Hall and the Constitution Center. In Memphis, the Rock & Soul Museum celebrates musical history, much of it from the town, but not the town itself. Italy is still focused on the hometown, not the country. (The only time Italian flags flap from windowsills is during soccer's World Cup.) Garibaldi may have united the geography, but a hundred and fifty years later, it's still not much of a country in the minds of the people.

On the way home we stop at the number two unifying element of the country (after soccer), the *gelateria*. Like most Italians, I can eat gelato every day. Coconut please, with bacio on top.

"Teresa, I read there's a new museum—the Museum of Gelato—not far from here. Have you two been there?" The four of us are enjoying our cool treat on a bench across the street.

She turns with an inquisitive look. "No, we haven't."

"Well, next time we visit, we'll have to go together." I scrape the last morsel from my paper cup. "Maybe they give samples!"

Mid-morning the next day we meet Louisa. She's staying downstairs in Christina's apartment. When the two women appear at the door, our friends wrap Louisa in their arms. An exuberant, auburn-haired woman in her forties, Louisa makes you feel like her favorite neighbor. Bustling around the apartment, she and Christina chatter like sisters. Between stories about her twins and travels, she's constantly teasing Giuliano and Teresa.

"You'll get to meet Maria Christina tonight," Louisa says to us after chiding Teresa for fussing too much over dinner. "You know, she's how I met G and T. Maria Christina, teaches English here, and she's a good friend of mine. Giuliano was her star pupil and so when I came for a visit, we had to get together with him and Teresa."

"She's responsible for us meeting them too," John says. "The teacher we contacted about finding an English speaker when we first moved here. Quite the matchmaker."

Louisa laughs. "G and T have adopted her as well."

I give her a conspiratorial look. "They have a tendency to do that."

Louisa's conversation bubbles around the room another half hour then she and Christina depart to pick up things for tonight's meal. John and I decide to go out for a stroll around the city. As we close the door, John calls, "We'll be back in plenty of time to help with dinner."

We wander through the crowded stalls of the Saturday market where you can buy a tablecloth, a winter jacket, a toaster, clothespins, a mortadella sandwich, hand-made jewelry, fresh fruit, or a leather belt. I loved shopping these markets when we lived in Italy so I drag John down row after row of stalls—just looking. We walk past our former Italian language school and stop into the coffee bar where the class would take a break each morning. "Remember our graduation day?" I say sipping my *macchiato*.

"Of course. I got to hug all the teachers." He leans toward me with a fake leer. "Especially Lucia."

95

My eyes roll. "Well it was so nice—the fuss they made every Friday for the graduates. Too bad it's Saturday, or we might have run into them."

In Piazza Maggiore we stop to admire the Neptune fountain, the place where we met Giuliano and Teresa nearly five years ago. "How about we walk back this way," John says, starting down Via Indipendenza on the opposite side. "We need to pick up some wine and we can swing by Garibaldi again."

A half hour later we've braved the stairs back to the Vitali apartment—with a few bottles of wine to add to the table. Teresa has dinner preparations underway. "What are you making?" I ask.

"Turkey cutlets." They're lightly coated with breadcrumbs and Teresa has lined a cookie sheet with parchment. She places about a tablespoon of butter under each cutlet, and a second tablespoon on top. Leeks and Belgian endive are cleaned and sitting on the kitchen table.

From the hallway we hear the door open and a clamor of voices fills the living room. Christina and husband, Paulo, son Alessandro, and Louisa. The women hurry to the kitchen with covered plates. Bread appears from a grocery bag and gets sliced into thin crostini. On the stove, leeks sauté in one pan, endive in another filling the air with a sweet, oniony aroma. By the time Maria Christina arrives to happy squeals from Louisa, Teresa has started the fried sage which adds another layer to the kitchen's fragrance. She stirs flour and club soda into a thin mixture and coats fresh sage leaves with it. Then they're dropped into a pot of hot oil. When they've browned sufficiently she drains them on paper towels. These are my favorites—crunchy and subtle tasting. Teresa and I made them together at our house in New Jersey, but I've never had much luck preparing them on my own.

The cutlets now cooked, Teresa tops each with thin slices of prosciutto and mozzarella and returns them to the oven for the cheese to melt. Huge capers dress both the leeks and Belgian endive. "I'd never think to serve leeks or endive like this," Louisa says to me as we carry dishes to the table.

In the kitchen, Christina is finishing the crostini and the green beans are cooked. Once the men have opened wine we all take our places around the table. First passed are the two plates of crostini. Crispy toasted baguette slices, one is spread with a creamy cheese, the other with some kind of pate. When the plates come my way, Alessandro, who's seated next to me, leans over and says, "I made those."

I sample the cheese one first. "This is delicious. So smooth."

I can tell he's proud. "It's not hard to make. I'll tell you."

The two of us connect easily around kitchen matters. Alessandro tells me he's now working in a seafood restaurant and we discover we both make *baccala*, the Italian salted cod John introduced me to years ago. Conversation flies around the table in three languages. Louisa speaks reasonable Italian, but lapses into Spanish, her parent's tongue, when she's stuck for a word. Maria Christina, who's more reserved than her American friend, translates some of the rapid Italian for us. *Garibaldi, who spoke all of these languages would be right at home at our table.* Giuliano tells everyone about our planned Sardinia visit. Louisa has stories about her fast-growing twins. We tell the others about our visit to the Bologna museum. Teresa beams from the compliments. Alessandro and his father lament with us about Italy's loss in the soccer championship.

"I brought all your favorites," Louisa announces. "I bought a used suitcase for ten dollars and filled it with maple syrup, Bisquick, powdered buttermilk—"

Cristina nearly shrieks her "GRAZIE!"

How funny is this? All of us hauling food across the Atlantic. I never thought Italians would want anything we have in our stores. Well, maybe maple syrup. *Is Christina going to make pancakes?*

It's late when we finally break up. Before he leaves, Alessandro tells me the recipe for the two crostini.

Parmigiano Toasts

3.5 ounces grated Parmigiano Reggiano

3.5 ounces cream

2 eggs

3.5 ounces milk

fresh ground pepper

Mix all ingredients in a blender. Put into a 350 degree oven for 5 minutes. Blend again and then put into the refrigerator. Spread on toasted baguette slices.

Mortadella Pate

1 thick slice (10.5 ounces) Italian mortadella
3.5 ounces sheep's milk ricotta
1 ounce grated Parmigiano Reggiano

In a hot skillet, cook the mortadella a few seconds on each side. Cool and dice. Put all ingredients into a blender or food processor. Mix until a paste is formed. Serve on toasted baguette slices.

This evening—as part of the Vitali international family—is one I'll always remember. Their friendship is the unexpected treasure of our time living here. You can travel to extraordinary places, visit all the museums, and eat the best food, but it's in the personal connections that you learn the truth of a place.

THE BLOOD OF ANGRY MEN

Our aim is to remake Italy into one independent sovereign nation of free men and equals. Young Italy proposes to reach these aims through education and insurrection. Education must always be directed to teach the need for insurrection by example, word and pen. Insurrection—by means of guerrilla bands—is the true method of warfare for all nations wanting to free themselves from foreign control.

GIUSEPPE MAZZINI, 1831

Avanti. Avanti. Save your bullets. Use your bayonet. Then pull the trigger. Watch your enemy die. Make him a hero. Avanti. Avanti.

GIUSEPPE GARIBALDI, 1849

ROME, ITALY

By the mid-1840s Giuseppe Mazzini's Young-Italy movement had spread to other parts of Europe where, seemingly overnight, there was a Young-France, Young-Hungary, Young-Poland, Young-Austria, and so on. Then, in 1848, Europe exploded. In February, Paris saw riots in the streets turn into outright revolution. By year end, French King Louis Philippe was overthrown, a Second Republic was formed, a constitution ratified, and Louis Napoleon was installed as president.

While not all the 1848 revolutions produced the dramatic changes seen in France, considerable freedoms were achieved. In both the Kingdom of Two Sicilies and the Kingdom of Sardinia-Piedmont, their monarchies agreed to govern in accordance to constitutions prescribed by elected legislators. Following a precedent set by Russia, Austria and Hungary abolished serfdom. The Netherlands installed a parliamentary democracy. And, Denmark ceased to be a monarchy altogether. Perhaps most impacted was the Austrian Empire where Ferdinand abdicated to his nephew, Franz Joseph, who at first agreed to liberal reforms but then spent much of the next two decades waging a fierce battle to rescind them.

With both Austria and France preoccupied in their own internal revolts, Giuseppe Mazzini declared a new Roman Republic, which immediately gained popular support by advocating the confiscation of large swaths of the Church's lands and redistribution to the poor. In Hungary, the Young Revolutionaries, led by Lajos Kossuth, were remarkably successful until Russian Tsar Nicholas I marched into Budapest with more than three hundred thousand troops to restore Franz Joseph's Habsburg government; Kossuth fled to exile in New York.

While Europe was on fire, the war in Uruguay was winding down. Britain and France, fearing for the lives of their own citizens living in Uruguay, used naval power to break the blockade of Montevideo. As part of a complex cease-fire, Britain induced the seventy-one-year-old Admiral Brown to accept retirement as a rear admiral in the British Navy at full pension; not to be outdone, Argentina not only made him rear admiral with full pension but also bestowed the title: Father of the Argentine Navy. Brown accepted all distinctions and retired to Buenos Aires where he died in 1857.

With Brown no longer a block, Garibaldi shipped Anita and their three surviving children to his mother in Nizza. On April 15th 1848, he and sixty-three loyal Red-Shirts followed on the *Speranza.* On December 11, all sixty-four brandishing ten-foot lances topped with streaming red-ribbons, entered Rome to fight for Mazzini's new Roman Republic.

Garibaldi, like Mazzini, saw Rome as the lynchpin to a unified Italy. Once Rome fell, they reasoned, the other territories would fall into place. But, Rome would prove to be Garibaldi's white whale. During his life, he would try and fail three times to win Rome. His first and best shot came in 1848. Paralleling Kossath's experience with Tsar Nicholas I, Garibaldi's early victories in Rome induced France's Louis Napoleon to employ overwhelming force to quash the revolution. Despite his ultimate defeat in Rome during this so-called First War of Independence, Garibaldi's brilliant tactics against superior forces would mark him forever as one of the three or four most prominent leaders of the movement to unify Italy, known as the Risorgimento.

In this era before photography, Rome attracted thousands of aspiring artists from all over Europe and beyond. Many paid for studies by selling images of tourist attractions painted *en plein air*, out in the open. These young artists, with their Bohemian ideas and rebellious ways, were immediately drawn to the charismatic Giuseppe Garibaldi and his multicultural Red Shirted followers— Brazilians, Blacks, Sicilians, English, Belgians, even one Frenchman. Garibaldi's army of volunteers would quickly grow to several thousand. Fearing the revolutionaries would overrun the city, Pope Pius IX fled to the fortress town of Gaeta located in the neighboring Kingdom of Two Sicilies.

Today, Nancy and I are in Rome to view the battlefield where Garibaldi would prove to the world that Italians could and would fight for freedom. I'm guessing we're within five hundred meters of the Janiculum summit. The sun is starting to cook. I'm anxious to get there before we fry. But, Nancy wants to reconnoiter. Her nose is stuck to the street map. She's so much better at directions than I. Then again, while she's exploring virtual Rome, I get to spend more time with the real thing.

"From here, we're supposed to see all seven hills," she says.

Legend holds that Romulus founded the original city on April 21st in 753 BC on the Palatine Hill and the seven hills were first occupied by small settlements. These were not grouped nor recognized as a city called Rome until the Servian Walls on the southeast boundary were constructed in the early 4th century BC. Of the seven hills of current Rome, five—the Aventine, Caelian, Esquiline, Quirinal, and Viminal—are populated with monuments, buildings, and parks. The Capitoline Hill now hosts Rome's city hall and its most important museums, and the Palatine Hill belongs to the main archaeological area.

We're staying on the west side of the Tiber (Tevere) in Trastevere which sits at the base of the Janiculum, known as the eighth hill of Rome. We arrived yesterday morning. Last night, we ate at Da Enzo where we enjoyed one of Nancy's favorite dishes, *burrata d'Andria*—served with fresh tomatoes and bread. We usually share dishes but whenever there's *burrata* on the menu, I know I have to order my own. We did share the *carbonara*. And those veal cutlets! Exquisite! To salve our conscience, this morning we only had coffee. No cornetto. But, all this walking is making me hungry again. For lunch, I want to go to Osteria der Belli, another of our favorites. I love their *frutti di mare*. But, first I want to find the exact spot where Garibaldi and his rag-tag army of volunteers beat back the French under General Oudinot.

"Italians will not fight."

That's what French General Oudinot said in 1849 when he landed with twelve thousand troops at Civitavecchia, the ancient port outside of Rome. Charged by Louis Napoleon with retaking Rome from Giuseppe Mazzini's handful of rabble, Oudinot had little doubt his troops would make quick work of their assignment. But, Oudinot was in for a big surprise. Giuseppe Garibaldi had assembled an army of eight thousand volunteers willing to fight, especially if the enemy were French.

When Garibaldi learned of Oudinot's epithet, he wrote this Order of the Day. *Repeat after me. Oh God grant me the grace that I may put all the steel of my bayonet inside a Frenchman and not deign to pull the trigger but keep my shot to kill a second Frenchman at not more than ten paces.*

In answer to the Pope's appeal for aid, Austria, Spain, Naples and France—all Catholic countries—had all agreed to send armies to restore the Pope in Rome. The French were the first to arrive. However, before Oudinot's forces could reach the walls of Rome, Garibaldi surprised them with a patchwork army of bolo-wielding gauchos, young artists, and fiercely independent Travesterites. The Italians drove the French from Janiculum Hill back to Civitavecchia, killing hundreds, and capturing over three hundred. Knowing reinforcements were on the way, Oudinot retreated and then called for a ceasefire. Garibaldi wanted to press the advantage but President Mazzini, believing the French wanted a diplomatic solution, gave the order to stop.

Meanwhile, Papal reinforcements kept coming. Austrians. Neapolitans. French. Eventually, Rome was surrounded. Artillery fire destroyed Villa Corsini; other buildings and parts of ancient Roman walls were severely damaged; residents were endangered.

By June, French and Austrian troops had breached the city walls. Mazzini, a practicing Catholic who believed in separation of church and state, continued to explore a diplomatic solution. He told the press, "the Pope's restoration would breed perpetual disquiet and conspiracies" against the papacy. American reporter, Margaret Fuller, echoed Mazzini by writing, "the Pope's action was bound to ignite sympathy and adhesion for the Republic." The French and Austrians continued their advance.

Though his forces were losing a battle of attrition, Garibaldi refused to surrender. Instead, he and a six-month pregnant Anita, who against his wishes, had joined him in Rome, urged his troops to escape in order to fight another day. Margaret Fuller recalled Garibaldi's passionate words:

Fortune, which today has betrayed us, will smile on us tomorrow. I am leaving Rome. Those of you who wish to continue the war against the foreigner should come with me. I cannot offer you pay, quarter or provision. I can only offer you hunger, thirst, forced marches, battles and death. Those who have Italy's name not only on your lips but in your hearts as well, must follow me.

"Yes, Honey," I say, "it's a great view. But, I want to get to the summit. Garibaldi's waiting. Anyway, I'll be damned if I can distinguish all seven hills."

"Garibaldi and his horse are not going anywhere," Nancy says. "Let's take a few minutes."

This is the third time we've stopped to admire the view. I have to admit, at each new high, the panorama of Rome gets better. Just across the river to the left is the tower of Castel Sant'Angelo where in Puccini's opera, *Tosca* escaped a bullet by jumping to her death. Below us, on this side of the river, I can see the red tile roof of our hotel.

Nancy hands me the binoculars, saying, "Follow your nose across the river. Can you see the Pantheon."

Shit! She's got to be kidding. Not long before we left, I had to get Avastin injections in both eyes. That was six weeks ago and the effect seems to be wearing off. Everything is starting to look like Dali paintings again. Shit! Shit!

"From there locate the Coliseum, Capitoline Hill and the Forum where Caesar got stabbed in the back."

"*Et tu Brute*," I say, changing the subject.

"Speaking of back stabbers," Nancy says, "there's the monument to one of your favorites. Can you see it?"

Looking right back at us is the so called Wedding Cake—the gleaming, overly large, overly garish, white monument to Vittorio Emmanuel II, King Vittorio. Credited with being the first king of a unified Italy, his reputation is about as inflated as his ugly monument—so prominent, even I can see it.

"Ah yes," I say. "If Marcus Antonio were here, I'm sure he'd want these present-day Romans to lend him their ears. You know, something along the lines of: Friends, Romans, and Countrymen, I come to bury Garibaldi, not to praise him. The evil that men do lives after them; the good is oft interred with their bones. King Vittorio says Garibaldi was ambitious, and Vittorio is an honorable man; et cetera, et cetera; yet when Garibaldi handed over all of south Italy to the future king, did Garibaldi seem ambitious? Et cetera, et cetera. Ambition should be made of sterner stuff. Et cetera, et cetera."

Nancy smiles, points at her map.

"Speaking of Garibaldi, this map says we're pretty much standing on the spot where he was wounded." That was on April 29th, 1849.

"What! Let me see."

Hmm, I wonder. Not enough cover here to be the spot. But, then again, in 1849, this place might have looked a lot different. More trees—either side of this clearing—forests, even—could be. Pines, most likely. This whole section must have been covered with pines—Italian pines—ones that look like giant lollipops—pines, like in Respighi's piece—the *Pines of Rome*. Nancy and I heard the Southwest Florida Symphony do it earlier this year. One of the four movements is called 'I Pini di Gianicolo' –the pines of Janiculum—written in 1918—it features a piccolo mimicking a singing nightingale. Beautiful. I wonder what Respighi would write today? The Park Benches of Gianicolo, featuring two teens sucking face? Who knows?

In 1849, the pines would have provided cover for Garibaldi's surprise attack. He had Bersiglieri marksmen hidden either side of the hill. When Garibaldi was hit, French troops rushed toward him. The marksmen opened up. And, bingo, Garibaldi turned defeat into victory—at least for that day.

"You could be right," I say to Nancy. "If so, this is where he was wounded in his side; the bullet's impact knocked him from his horse. This is where Andrea Aguyar—his giant bodyguard, the former slave—came to Garibaldi's rescue. Aguyar used his ten-foot lance to cut down a French trooper ready to fire a kill shot into the wounded GG. This could very well be the spot."

I'm still not totally convinced. These local maps can't be trusted. Plus, we're in spitting distance from a church not mentioned in any of the accounts of the battle. Nancy's map says the church is San Pietro di Montorio, built in 1509; it supposedly marks the exact spot where Saint Peter was crucified, died and ascended into heaven. In other words, this is an important historical monument. So, either we've got the battle location wrong, or Garibaldi used the little church as cover for his wild bayonet charge.

Walking towards the church, I say to Nancy. "It doesn't completely add up."

We're now within ten feet of an attractive white-haired woman painting *en plein air.* She says in an English accent, "Oh, it's only a legend."

"Garibaldi' s attack?" I say.

"Oh, I'm sorry. I thought you were speaking about Saint Peter. There's no real evidence Saint Peter was crucified here. But, it makes for a great story. The Italians love their myths."

She makes a good point. That Garibaldi was a real hero is indisputable. Wounded eight times, captured and escaped more times than Houdini, sea captain, buccaneer, cowboy, general, Hero of Two Worlds. His accomplishments speak for themselves. Yet, there are myths that would have you believe he was some sort of superhuman.

"I'm starting a new myth," I say. "We all know Garibaldi was a virulent anti-papist. I can see his mind working now. I'll stop the bastards who would restore the Pope to Rome at the very spot where Christ's first Pope, Peter the Rock, ascended into heaven. Pure Garibaldi, eh? See the irony? This is the spot."

Nancy and the English artist are gawking at me like I'm some kind of crazed lunatic. Nancy smiles. "Oh, it's ironic alright. Look over here. Look at this street sign."

The sign says Via Garibaldi. The church of Saint Peter of Montorio is on Via Garibaldi.

Now the three of us are laughing. Saint Peter was crucified, died and ascended into heaven on a street the Italians have named after the Pope's number one adversary, Giuseppe Garibaldi. Now, that's irony!

"Okay," Nancy says, "let's go to the summit."

Walking along we spot an equestrian statue. It's Garibaldi, all right, but not Giuseppe; it's Anita. She's riding a galloping horse with a pistol in her right hand and holding her newborn child in her other. It's a striking monument, which in my view, gives voice to those who would deflate the Garibaldi legend by exaggeration. The truth is, Anita was not in Rome for any of the fighting. She arrived as Garibaldi was preparing his escape.

Leaving Anita's monument, we take Viale Aldo Fabrizi for about one hundred meters where we come to a large piazza. This is the Janiculum summit, and I'm looking at an enormous equestrian statue of Giuseppe Garibaldi. The statue, designed by Emilio Gallori and erected in 1895, sits atop a large pedestal depicting both the battle and allegorical scenes. An inscription on the plinth reads '*Roma o Morte*,' Rome or Death.

"Funny thing about that statue," I say.

"What?" Nancy asks.

"It's positioned with his horse's ass pointed toward the Vatican."

SANCTUARY CITIES

After being marooned by terrified boatmen on the islet called Villa di Comacchio, she was conveyed to a dairy farm at Mandriole. There she died. Garibaldi, whose calm strength had for months borne up to a sea of troubles, now broke down utterly and wept like a child.

F.J. SNELL, *THE STORY OF GARIBALDI AND THE ITALIAN UNIFICATION*

SAN MARINO

It isn't a typical sign. As we round yet another bend in the zig zag road up the mountainside, a green lawn occupies the inside of the curve. In the middle a three-foot hedge forms the words *Benvenuto San Marino*. Welcome. Beside it, planted in flowers, is the crest of San Marino, the fifth smallest country in the world. Surrounded by Italy, it claims to be the world's oldest surviving sovereign state. The street map of this country, shown on a roadside poster, looks like a long piece of spaghetti draped back and forth, back and forth across an oblong plate.

"We could have taken the cable car," says Teresa, "but you'd miss seeing the residential area below the old city." As usual, she and her husband are making sure we get the most out of today's drive. We're headed to the Center where the Christmas market is.

"Bet Garibaldi would have appreciated the cable car," I say. "Not quite the way he arrived, is it?"

John picks up his cue. "Not at all. It was 1849 and he was on the run. Escaping from Rome through mountainous terrain with the French and Austrians on his tail. Most of his four thousand men were captured or killed. Aguilar, the former slave and close friend who had fought with him in Uruguay, was among them. Ugo Bassi had been captured. Anita, pregnant and sick with malaria, was extremely ill. Garibaldi was afraid of being surrounded."

"But he found refuge here, right?"

"Not exactly. He asked for it, but since San Marino was neutral, the regent said they couldn't stay—unless the men disarmed. Garibaldi left some of his men behind and fled north."

On our left the high wall of the old city fortress appears. We pull off on the right for a panoramic view of the valley, the opposite hilltops poking through a thick mist. Near the crest of the mountain, Giuliano parks the car. As we walk through one of the squares I notice a huge bronze plaque on the wall. It's written in Italian, French, and thankfully, English and I read for all of us. "It says San Marino has been an independent republic since the 13th century." At the end of the narrow street we climb the stairs to the top of the old fortress wall where the Christmas market is set up. Small log chalets line one side of the wide battlement, each with red-draped counters in front of the central opening displaying their wares—oils and marmalades, honey, jewelry, wine, sweaters, capes and woolen hats, holiday decorations and simple toys. A ten-foot Santa stilts his way through the crowd and nearby a juggler balances one of his batons on his nose to amuse clapping children.

"Come look at this," I say pulling John's sleeve toward an unusual booth.

On a table there's a model of the San Marino mountain, five tiers high with a stair winding from bottom to top, all of it made from tree bark. Smaller examples, little three- and four-tiered villages, are for sale. In another booth we find a *presepe*, the Italian nativity scene, depicted as a rocky mountain village with model houses, barns, shepherds, running sheep, and the Holy Family shown gathered in a cave beneath an angel.

At a vendor with beautifully made leather goods John and I buy a wallet and gloves. Teresa chooses two dolls for Louisa's twins and a scarf for one of her grandsons. Drawn by the smoky aroma, we pick up paper cones of roasted chestnuts that warm my fingers. A narrow, steep street leads towards the main piazza. Near its entrance another bronze plaque, with the name Garibaldi on it, catches my attention. Someone has rubbed out a word and replaced it with *tedeschi*, Germans. The first part indicates this is the house where on July 31, 1849, Garibaldi...the rest of the language is puzzling. "Giuliano, what does it mean?"

"It says Garibaldi thanked San Marino's regent for his help, but did not surrender to the Germans (Austrians) keeping hope for the future."

"Pretty incredible that we stumbled on this," John says. "Funny how we find Garibaldi references everywhere."

"Hey, give me some credit here," I say with false indignation. "You're always saying I wander off too much. But *I'm* the one who finds all this cool stuff."

The town/country's main piazza has a long overlook bookended by two municipal buildings. Palazzo Publico, the town hall with its clock tower, looks like a miniature of Florence's Palazzo Vecchio. A bell tower tops the building on the opposite end. Over the doorway of each is the blue-and-white flag of the country. The fog is burning off now and we have a better view of the valley below, but after a few minutes Giuliano wants us to head back to the car. We have another stop to make.

Retracing our route over the zig zag road, we turn northeast, following the path of Garibaldi's escape. He was heading for Venice but along the way, tragedy struck his life again. He and his soldiers escaped to Cesenatico. The tiny fishing village, once a major shipping port, is close to our friends' home in Cervia, so they've been there often.

"You won't believe what you'll see there tonight," Teresa says eagerly. "It's a very special Christmas display."

Once we reach the town Giuliano leads the way to one of their favorite restaurants. As we often do when our friends choose a locale, we ask him to order for all of us. When our antipasti arrives John and I are speechless. The waiter places a wooden pizza board on the table laden with prosciutto, salami, big chunks of mortadella, olives, fresh mozzarella, thick bread slices topped with melted cheese and spinach, tomato-topped focaccia, crispy chips, big spinach rolls, and a sort of quesadilla stuffed with eggplant. A basket of thin, grilled bread arrives too.

"This is the *appetizer?*" John says, reaching for a chunk of the mortadella. We all dig in and by the time our pasta arrives, we've pretty much cleaned off the pizza board. Over dinner we learn about what's in store.

"The Marine Museum is unique in Italy," says Giuliano. "There's a small museum building of course, but the real exhibit is the boats."

"There are ten of them," says Teresa, "All lined up in the canal. The kind of boats Garibaldi used for his escape."

"The canal was designed by Leonardo da Vinci. Cesare Borgia had asked him to find a solution to the silting problem," adds Giuliano.

"Really?" I say, "Leonardo."

Teresa continues. "In summer the sails are hoisted on all the boats, beautiful sails. Geometric designs in red and yellow-gold. Many have emblems of the fishing families who owned them. We've gone there a few times for the Garibaldi Festival when the boats are sailed out into the Adriatic, and the town is full of red-shirts. It's quite a sight." *Too bad we aren't here for that.*

It's dark when we exit the restaurant and stroll toward the museum. Rounding a corner we see the surprise. Floating in the still waters of the canal, the decks of all ten boats are flooded with light. Robed mannequins fill each of them. Tiny lights outline the triangular shapes of the sails. Above the largest boat, at the head of the canal, the outline of a star hovers over the tallest sail. Everything is mirrored in the still water doubling the glimmering effect.

I draw my breath. "How beautiful!"

As we approach the large boat I can make out the scene aboard—a nativity, complete with shepherds and the offering from the kings. From the mast of the enormous front sail, an angel spreads her arms in welcome.

"That must be the biggest *precepe* in all of Italy," John says.

"The display is here from the beginning of December until Epiphany," says Giuliano as we amble along the canal. Other boats show the life of the people during the holiday season—fishermen pulling their nets, musicians, and children watching a puppet show. Pale, yellow lamps shed soft illumination on the quay. In the canal, the twenty lighted "sails" all pointing the same direction, their twin reflections in the water, this scene would have inspired Van Gogh. Giuliano points to the boat at the head of the canal. "That biggest boat is a *bragozzo*. The rest are called *luggers*, the typical ships of the north Adriatic."

John walks closer to the waterside to look at the carvings on the bow of the *bragozzo*. "I can imagine this one, filled with Garibaldi's troops when he sailed for Venice on August second. Cesenatico was one of the main ports of the Adriatic at the time and the only place he could find enough boats for their escape. I think he had about ten or twelve of them when he left—all that were available."

"But he didn't get far, did he?" I say.

"Austrian ships intercepted them and they had to run inland. They kept heading north, but had to stop the next day because Anita's malaria had turned much worse. They found shelter with a farm family near Ravenna. That's where his beloved wife died in his arms the night of August fourth. Garibaldi was beside himself with grief."

"That's so sad," Teresa says.

John nods. "His comrades encouraged him to keep going, and so, after a hurried burial in the woods, they moved on."

A few years later her body was recovered and moved to a cemetery in town. Then, in 1859, Garibaldi had her moved to his family plot in Nice. But she wouldn't rest yet. In 1932, Mussolini was trying to wrap himself in a Garibaldi cloak. He erected the gun-wielding, galloping statue to Anita in Rome—and moved her body under it, usurping Garibaldi's wishes while claiming to "honor" him.

NEW YORK, NEW YORK

After his exile from Italy in 1849, Garibaldi, like so many of his comrades-in-arms,
had attempted to start life over again as a civilian. He arrived in the United States on
July 30, 1850. The city of New York offered him public honors and a stipend, but he
refused; instead he found work in a candle factory owned by an Italian called Meucci.

ANDREA VIOTTI, *GARIBALDI, THE REVOLUTIONARY AND HIS MEN*

STATEN ISLAND, NEW YORK

Look at me. I'm in Garibaldi's bedroom, brandishing his actual battle saber, shouting his famous words when he landed in Sicily: "Here we make Italy, or die."

Nancy puts down the camera and says "You know, as your beard gets whiter,
you're starting to look like Garibaldi. If you were wearing a red shirt instead of a
blue blazer, and a rep tie, people might mistake you for the man himself."

I'm flattered but I think to myself how different Garibaldi's life and times
were from mine. Yes, I have had my modest share of accomplishments. The son
of Sicilian immigrants, college educated, world traveler, entrepreneur, bestsell-
ing author, Nancy's husband; some might consider me an American success
story. But, let's face it: Compared to Garibaldi, my life has been pretty dull. To
paraphrase Senator Lloyd Bentsen in his debate with Dan Quayle: *Mr. Petralia, I*
served with Garibaldi; Garibaldi was a friend of mine: and, Sir, you're no Garibaldi.

I get it there's a big difference between overthrowing the Kingdom of Naples and winning a seventies-plus tennis tournament or scoring tickets for *Kinky Boots*. I've never had to endure any the hardships he did: Going to sea in a square rigger for months, even years; eking out an existence; living off the land; fighting hand to hand; looking into the eyes of an enemy while ripping out his guts; being shot eight times; captured; imprisoned; tortured; losing a wife in battle. He's credited with saving a dozen people from drowning. When I fell off our nineteen-foot sloop into Barnegat Bay, Nancy had to save me. But, for me, for us, being asked to speak at this museum is a big deal. Think what you want, we're feeling honored and proud.

This is our second visit to the Muecci cottage on Staten Island where Garibaldi lived. Listed on the U.S. National Register of Historic Places as the Garibaldi-Muecci Museum, their brochure says its members' mission is *to collect, preserve and exhibit material relating to the lives of inventor Antonio Muecci and legendary hero Giuseppe Garibaldi and to conduct cultural, artistic and educational programs and classes to promote the understanding of Italian-American heritage.*

Garibaldi, exiled for the second time in his life, arrived in New York July 30, 1850 where local Italians were raising funds to buy him a merchant ship. In the meantime, he needed a place to live and a way to earn a living to support his mother and four children living in Nice. His hosts became Ester and Antonio Muecci, Italian immigrants who owned a small candle making business on Staten Island. The initial plan was for Garibaldi to apply for U.S. citizenship while working as a candle maker. This scheme would free up Antonio to work on his real passion: electricity. However, when funds for the merchant ship fizzled in the spring of 1851, Garibaldi signed on as sea captain on the three-mast Peruvian schooner, *Carmen* sailing to Lima. From Lima, he made several voyages carrying bat guano, fertilizer, to Hong Kong, Canton, Manila, Australia, New Zealand and back to New York. These voyages provided sufficient funds for him to care for his family and to begin plans for a return to Europe in November 1853 for yet another shot at unification.

While Garibaldi was traveling the world, Antonio Muecci was experimenting with electrical currents to treat pain. That's when he discovered sound, in this case a man's scream, could be heard through the wires connected from the screamer's mouth to his own. His invention, which he later called the talking telegraph, pre-dated Alexander Graham Bell's by twenty-something years. As with most events associated with Garibaldi, Muecci's triumph would not have a happy ending. Worried others might steal his invention, Muecci never sought a patent. Instead, he continued to perfect his talking telegraph up until the time Bell was granted a patent for the telephone. As the legal inventor of the telephone, Bell became world renowned and rich; Muecci, like Garibaldi, died in poverty.

The first time we came to this museum three years ago, we were tourists. This time, we are here by invitation. Museum director, Marianna Randazzo has asked us to speak about our book, *Not in a Tuscan Villa*, and to discuss our current project, *Looking for Garibaldi*. Because we now live in Florida, a trip to New York requires a bit of planning. We were not going to fly from Fort Myers to New York without spending a couple of days enjoying the city and visiting with friends.

So, on this trip, we're staying with good buddies, Sy and Susan, at their lovely home in Westfield, NJ, a hop skip into Manhattan. Yesterday afternoon the four of us popped into the "City" for a full day of activities. First stop: Washington Square. Why? You guessed it: To see the Garibaldi statue, of course. That's right, in addition to the Muecci-Garibaldi Museum on Staten Island, New Yorkers have a prominent statue *on the Square* of Garibaldi posed—no other way to say it: awkwardly—reaching for his sword. Completed in 1885, the Garibaldi figure had been designed by artist Giovanni Turni to stand on an irregular rock, not a flat surface. But the pedestal and the figure were cast in different foundries. When a rock-less pedestal was delivered to the site, the Italian patrons who commissioned the work had run out of funds. As an expedient, their leader told foundry workers to simply reshape Garibaldi's left leg so it would reach the flat base. Upon seeing the finished product, Turini called the person who ordered the change "a cruel amputator."

From Washington Square, the four of us headed over to Central Park to have an early dinner at Villagio, a newer Italian restaurant Nancy discovered last year. Thrilled we could introduce Sy and Susan to a place in their back yard, we enjoyed excellent service and great food all in time to get to the theater to see *Kinky Boots.* Great show.

"John, Nancy, people are arriving. We should go downstairs. Meet some of our members. Get ready for your talk." It's Marianna's nice way of saying, *John, you should not be touching the exhibits. Please return the saber to the bed. Come with me.*

Save for its namesakes, there is nothing extraordinary about the Garibaldi-Muecci house. That is to say, we will be speaking in a living room, not an amphitheater. Crowded in are about forty people sitting on folding chairs. About half are holding our book, *Not in a Tuscan Villa.* We'll sign them later. Right now, we're being introduced by Marianna. *Kind words. Much appreciated.* She also mentions we have books to sell. Again, much appreciated. I interrupt. "All proceeds from our book sale today will go to the museum. So, if any of you want to pay a little more, no one will object. Not even Garibaldi." I get a laugh. Marianna is surprised. She thanks us.

Off to a good start, I begin our talk with a discussion about our motivation to live in Italy for exactly one year. Why? We were looking for an adventure. It was a way to hone our language skills. A challenge? Yes, indeed. It was not always easy. Yes, we did have problems. We did not like our first apartment. We had to break our lease. The visa process was hellish. We were in Italy as tourists but the authorities treated us like immigrants. I had a detached retina that required an emergency operation. None of these obstacles could mar the overall experience. Suffice it to say when our year was up, we didn't want to leave. On the plane back to the states, we cried. Why did we leave? Our visa expired.

For my reading, I've selected a chapter in our book where Nancy and I begin to discover facts about Garibaldi that pique our interest to write the book you're now reading. Known as the Hero of Two Worlds, in his day he was one of the world's best known people. After helping to unify Italy, in 1861, he almost became a general in Lincoln's Union Army.

For Nancy and me, part of the fun of living in Italy was bumping into all things Garibaldi. From our apartment in Parma, we took trains all over the mainland. The great thing about Italy is the diversity of geography, foods, and micro-climes among towns. Nonetheless, in every town there are constants: More churches than priests, more old people than teens, and always some sort of tribute to the great Giuseppe Garibaldi.

Nancy is up next. Instead of immediately reading a chapter as I did, she engages the audience with a few questions? How many here have been to Italy? *Almost everybody.* How many would like to live there for an extended period? *Almost everybody.* Anybody, like me, not Italian? Several people raise their hands. Anybody speak Italian? *Almost everybody.* A woman identifies herself as an Italian teacher. She's read the book. *Liked it. Wonders if dialects were a problem for us.* Nancy says "All Italian is a problem for me, especially the dialects. Napoli is the worst. There, everybody makes Italian sound like Russian." She gets a laugh, goes on to read a few paragraphs from a section called *Living in a Foreign Language* and then segues into a chapter called *La Famiglia.* It tells about meeting my cousins in Trieste and Padua. Pow. Instant connection. Like opening a spigot, a roomful of reminisces come pouring out. A woman tells of visiting her mother's village in Sicily. *They knew me immediately. Remembered my mom. Said I looked just like her. They forced fed me until I was about to burst. I loved it.* A man relates a similar story about visiting cousins in Calabria. Two sixty-something sisters chime in by relating how they discovered secrets about their own father while visiting his hometown in Lazio. *Can't tell you. Too embarrassing.*

More stories. The whole room is buzzing in two languages. I'm stuttering and laughing at the same time. Can't help myself. I put my arm around Nancy and hug.

FOREVER LOST

We have to distrust each other, it's our only defense against betrayal.

TENNESSEE WILLIAMS

COMO, ITALY

John and I disembark the ferry at the southern edge of Lake Como in the city of the same name. On this early summer day there's a chilly breeze coming off the water but the city sparkles in the sunlight. Unlike the steep hillsides of the northern towns along the lake we've been visiting, Como nestles on a flat plain between the mountains. *Exploring here should be easier than I thought.* Julius Caesar established the town in the first century BC, draining a swampy area next to the lake and moving the town down from the hills. *Imagine that. I wonder if Caesar, like me, liked inhabiting a flat terrain.* You've got to admire the Romans. Incredible engineers. *How did they drain the swamp?* But after their demise all that knowledge was lost for more than a thousand years.

We stroll along the waterfront where a wide park separates the road from the lake, and trees shade both the park and sidewalks. A mix of handsome buildings in shades of yellow, beige and pink lines the street, their windows and doors shut tight against the brisk air. Restaurant awnings flap over the sidewalks where the Italian patrons, scarves knotted tight against their throats, ignore the breeze. Crossing an enormous piazza lined with trees and shrubs, we follow pedestrian-only streets filled with locals and their young children, twenty-somethings sporting backpacks, touring families and seniors. For a few blocks we trail a group and their English-speaking guide, eavesdropping on her story of the city's Roman origins, and arrive at the *duomo*. Its flat facade is unusual with columns of statues stacked like shoeboxes from ground level to roof. Over the recessed, arched doorframe more statues flank tall, narrow, stained-glass windows. Many of these sculptures depict historical characters, including famous Romans. On either side of a giant rose window, two square recesses hold the statues of Pliny the Elder and Pliny the Younger, both of whom were born here.

Beyond the *duomo*, we meander the pleasant streets. "That's the fifth or sixth shoe store we've seen in the last two blocks," I say to John as he pauses to admire soft soccer models. "Do you think they manufacture them here?"

"Maybe. Funny, isn't it, how Italian cities are famous for certain products. Parma for ham and cheese, Florence for leather products—"

"Venice for glass. Modena for balsamic—"

"For bicycles and Ferraris too." *His interest.*

"Perugia for chocolates." *That's mine.*

"So maybe Como is famous for shoes. Do you want to look for some?"

I shake my head. "Not really. Let's just keep going. We need to find Garibaldi before we head back." John gives a last, longing glance at the soccer shoes. He's nearly as bad as I when it comes to shoes. Maybe it's his aging feet that have spread, but I suspect it's more his sense of style, his desire to be hip, that's filled his shoe cubbies to overflowing.

We find traces of the Roman settlement Caesar built—the streets laid out in a grid, many of them surprisingly wide. Shops with clothing, shoes, and jewelry intersperse with trattorias, and tiny bars. Bouquets in the entrance to a floral shop scent the air when we pass. Like the other lake towns, greenery is abundant, even deep into the ancient center. Above the street level, flowers dangle from windowsills and a surprising number of trees and shrubs are growing in pots and on balconies. Verdant vines obscure ancient stone archways. People stroll the streets and lounge in cafes, but it's nothing like the crowds of more popular cities. In the narrow passageways, blocked by the sun, it feels colder. Before long I'm pulling my windbreaker tighter and rubbing my arms. "Can we stop for a coffee?"

On a wide avenue we find a bar with red tablecloths topping their outdoor tables. John goes inside for our *caffè* while I turn my face to the sun's warmth. He returns a few minutes later with my favorite—cappuccino. Above us, the balconies are overflowing with greenery all along the street. At the end of it, about a block away, an imposing, five-story stone tower dominates the surrounding buildings. A large arched opening at the bottom stretches nearly the entire width and over it are four floors of open twin arches.

"What do you think that is?" John says taking a bite of the *cornetto* he bought to accompany his Americano.

"I think it's probably Porta Torre. I read something about it last night. Built, maybe, in the 12th century to protect the city's most important entrance. Let's check it out when we've finished."

A few minutes later we approach the wide, open archway and cross under. From inside, we can look up to the sky. Wooden floors and roof must have burned long ago. This was a military building. *I wonder how they used those open arches on the city side. Observation of the city? Portals for supplies? To waive a flag of victorious celebration? Or a spot to hurl an enemy to his death? Incidents like that weren't uncommon in the Middle Ages.* On the opposite wall we can see two more arches open to the outside. "Let's walk through. See what's on the other side," I say.

"Odd isn't it," John says when we exit. "The outside wall is solid and then you have those four floors of open arches on the inside."

"I know. The article didn't say why."

The medieval wall still attaches to one side of the tower, running about twelve feet high all along the street. An enormous piazza flanks the wall about fifty yards away. In its center a circular grassy area the size of a city block surrounds a tall monument.

John looks up at the street sign and smiles. "It's Piazza Vittoria. Victory. Let's go see that statue."

We can't help laughing when we get close. We've found him—Giuseppe Garibaldi. He looks young in his round cap, his face turned with determination in the direction of Austria. A heavy cloak covers him to below the knees and he's gathered it somewhat with his left hand. His right hand, extended backwards in preparation, clutches a saber. Someone has tied a long, red, knit scarf around his neck and it dangles below his waist barely swaying in the thin cool breeze.

"That's pretty neat," John says when we get close. "I guess he's still recognized as a hero here."

"What's the scene in bronze at the base of the monument? Looks like him with his troops on one side. That other fellow is handing him something."

"'*Alla riscossa populare del marzo 1859.*' It means the retaking of the area. They're probably turning over the keys to the city. It was an important victory—the start of the Second War of Independence. His second chance at creating a unified Italy. This time the Kingdom of Piedmont and Sardinia was battling the Austrians who had crossed into Piedmont."

"A second chance. And his dream appeared possible. He must have been really pleased."

"But in true Garibaldi form, it turned to another personal tragedy. Piedmont and France were the victors so they got the spoils. In the ensuing peace with the Austrians, they divided the territory. Lombardy became part of the Kingdom of Sardinia, and France got—Nice."

"His birthplace went back to *France?*"

"Right."

Imagine that. You fight off an army that's invaded your homeland—the "country" where you were born. Then, when the dust settles, the town you grew up in is now part of somebody *else's* country. Actually it was more than his hometown. Nizza was a province on the French border so it was a natural target for French acquisition. I know political negotiations are tricky. Everyone's got to come away feeling like a winner. But Garibaldi *was* the winner. How could the king be so callous to slight his general like that? Couldn't he have found something else to give away? Genoa maybe.

THE MESSIAH ARRIVES

I am not afraid of death. What I am afraid of is that I will meet the Saviour and He will say, "You could have done better."

GIUSEPPE GARIBALDI

PALERMO, ITALY

In 1860, Garibaldi and a thousand Red Shirts boarded two ships in Genoa, sailed to Sicily, and defeated the combined armies of the Kingdom of Two Sicilies. This incredible David/Goliath victory was followed by a series of negotiations, plebiscites and treaties. By 1871, even the Pope acquiesced when the Papal States became part of a unified Italy. With the last piece of the puzzle in place, Italy's version of Manifest Destiny became realized and Giuseppe Garibaldi could add Unifier of Italy to his impressive list of monikers which already included Hero of Two Worlds, Admiral, General, and El Diablo.

Our plan is to drive west to Marsala, spend the night. Tomorrow, we'll look for the exact spot where the two ships, Piemonte and Lombardo, landed with Garibaldi's Thousand Redshirts on May 11, 1860. I'm particularly interested in finding the hill at Calatafimi where Garibaldi led an uphill bayonet charge uttering his famous exultation: *Qui si fa l'Italia o si muore,* Here we make Italy, or we die. But, first we'll have to get through town.

121

Taking the overnight ferry here from Rome seemed a good idea. Our rented red Ford Fiesta is packed. We're ready to explore. The streets, however, have their own agenda. Nancy shouts, "The GPS says turn left." But, the street sign displays the unmistakable slash-circle icon telling us do not enter. We continue uphill. Next intersection, same thing. No left turn. Continuing up the hill may be a good tactic if we want to reconnoiter the territory or perhaps recreate a bayonet charge but it's not where we want to go. At the next intersection, there's a street that will put us back on our route but a truck is stopped, blocking entry while the driver unloads cases of Crodini soda. People here need their pick-me-up. He's not moving for anyone. When I slow down to evaluate my alternatives, the line of cars behind me honks like crazy. I open my window to ask a vendor for directions. As I lean my head out the window, I am nearly decapitated by a shirtless teenager zipping through traffic on a Honda, not the requisite Vespa mind you, but a full blown Honda motorcycle. I think to myself: Large bike, little bastard. The vendor is now shoving pears into my face. I can't get my question out. He assesses me as a total idiot, mumbles something inaudible, spits to the side, and quickly turns away to serve real customers. The driver in the car behind me, is all screams and arm waving. Pedestrians are staring at me. Everyone around our car is frowning, mouthing, pointing at us. I feel like Donald Sutherland in the scene from *The Body Snatchers* when people around him realize he is not a pod and they all start pointing and screaming *laaaalalalalalalaaaa*. I hit the gas, move another ten meters, run into more of the same. Raise the windows. Body snatchers are everywhere.

Welcome to Palermo!

It was Palermo where Garibaldi and his red-shirted volunteers won important early battles against a better-equipped professional army numbering over twenty thousand. It was in this harbor, the Palermo harbor, this stinking traffic-jammed Palermo harbor, where Garibaldi, on the British ship Hannibal, received articles of surrender from the Royalist defenders, where the Sardinian ship Maria Adelaide acknowledged his feats with a nineteen-gun salute, where Sicilian priests who knew him to be a papist-hating, anti-religious dictator defiantly celebrated holy masses in his honor, where a Royalist bullet ricocheted off his pistol and struck his foot, where in hand to hand combat he decapitated an enemy officer about to bayonet a Red Shirt, where he allowed Royalist troops to evacuate with all honors of war, where so many of his finest young followers gave their last full measure, where he would deliver a eulogy so eloquent the survivors were said to envy the fallen, where English woman Jesse White Mario worked tirelessly to nurse hundreds of wounded at a makeshift dockside hospital, where his great friend in arms, General Tukory, perished from multiple wounds, where even his biggest doubters began to believe a united Italy just might become a reality, where people knelt in the streets, touched his stirrups, made the sign of the cross, kissed his hands, where children were held up towards him as before a saint, and where women lined the streets to throw flowers in his path, where Alexander Dumas would come in his personal yacht to meet him, dine with him, write about him, and where Victor Hugo would write these words:

Grand are the liberators of mankind! Let them hear the grateful applause of nations. Yesterday we gave our tears; today our hosannas are heard. John Brown failed in America but Garibaldi has triumphed in Europe. Mankind shuddering at the infamous gallows of Charles Town, takes courage once more at the flashing sword of Calatafimi.

Hopelessly stymied in traffic, looking down over the city, I allow my mind to freestyle scenes from that other day. Dumas likened it to Christ entering Jerusalem. I can see it. Hadn't I witnessed something similar right in front of my home on South 18th Street in Philadelphia? It was June 1960, one hundred years after Garibaldi's triumphant parade through Palermo. I had just celebrated my twentieth birthday, still one year shy of being able to vote for the president. I had completed my sophomore year in college. My summer job entailed shift work at the Rohm and Haas chemical plant in Northeast Philly. My sleep time was day time. Nodding off on the job could get a temp like me fired. I had worked the previous night. I should have been in bed, asleep. But, on this morning, I was charged up; we were to have a special visitor. My father and three brothers, occupied with work or chores, were not home. But, mom was prepared. Earlier that morning, she had collected roses from our yard. Now they were a bowl of petals. Pink petals. The Democrat candidate for the presidency of the United States, young, handsome, war hero, Irish Catholic—not an Italian Catholic, but close enough—was going to pass in front of our house and my Sicilian mother was armed with pink rose petals.

"Mom, the Secret Service guys will never let you get close enough to throw the petals," I said. Mom paid me no mind. Mom was on a mission.

Our two local motorcycle cops, both called Wild Bill, dressed in black leather, came roaring up 18th Street. I knew both cops well. But, this was the first and only time I had ever seen them together. Usually they worked separate shifts. This was a special day. "Stay on the sidewalks. No one in the street," shouted Wild Bill Cohen. Seconds later, came Wild Bill Tumolo: "He's at Porter Street. The motorcade will be by here in two minutes."

Mom and I are standing on the top step of our row house. I can see him coming. Standing, waving in an open car, he is heading straight for us. As if drawn by magnet, mom moves from our steps to the sidewalk. His car is now only about fifty yards away. "Mom, Mom, where are you going?"

She heads into the street. Motor cycle cops—not the Wild Bills—not cops from our forty-eighth precinct—cops we do not know—shout at her. "Lady, get back!" Mom is undeterred. I have to stop her. She is going to get hurt. I reach her the exact moment the motorcade reaches us. He is right there, a few feet from us. As he moves by, Mom fires. Pink rose petals. My Sicilian mother covers the visitor in rose petals. For me, the replay unfolds in slow motion. The right hand brushing petals from his hair. Click. The turn. Click. The surprised look. Click. A smile. Click. A chuckle. Joy. Click. His lips forming words. Click. And, then, with a nod of his head—"Thank you." We all hear it. Everyone around us hears it. "Thank you."

Then everything speeds up. He is getting away. I run after the motorcade. I run past the foreign cops. Run right up to him, extended my hand, shouting "Jack. Jack." And Jack, scores of pink rose petals dotting his pin-striped, navy-blue suit, grabs my hand, shakes it, looks directly at me, and again says, "Thank you." Senator John F. Kennedy, future president of the United States, shakes my hand, and—thanks me. Click.

"Go! Go!" Nancy is shouting. "Stop day dreaming and drive. Let's get to the hotel before dark."

SWEET DISCOVERIES

There are no strangers here; Only friends you haven't yet met.

WILLIAM BUTLER YEATS

CONVERSANO, ITALY

After a one hour flight we pick up a car at the Bari airport and find our way to Conversano. I've selected this centrally located castle town on a Pugliese "hill" as the base for our exploration of Italy's heel. We want to learn what the people here think of Garibaldi and the Risorgimento.

Our landlady's brother, Giuseppe, meets us at a petrol station and shows us where to park. Trailing noisy bags, we rumble under a high stone archway and down a pedestrian street to the old stone house we've rented in the ancient part of town. Wider than normal, each floor has two windows facing the narrow passageway, their polished walnut shutters open to the light. On the lower floor, the windows have narrow, iron balconies crowned with flowers. *Perfect*. Inside it's charming, stocked with lovely linens and comfortable beds. After our tour of the house and our business transactions, we walk back through the arch with Giuseppe.

Opposite the archway a stone-paved, pedestrian street about forty feet wide stretches past restaurants and curves around the base of the castle. From here it looks more like a hodgepodge of architectural add-ons than a castle, although on one end a faceted structure with a bric-a-brac top stands like an enormous squat chess piece. Lined with trees and benches on the opposite side, the street drops off to a hillside park where some boys are kicking a water-filled jumbo soda bottle across the stone pavement of a modern amphitheater. The *crack!* and clatter of their ersatz soccer ball punctuates their excited voices. Around the perimeter two girls circle their bikes.

"You know where to park now," Giuseppe says in Italian pulling me back from my observations. "Over there behind that building you won't have to pay. There's a good pizzeria just up those steps behind you."

I make a mental note of the restaurant's sign. We have no groceries as yet. "And the market?" I ask.

"Just over there," he says gesturing toward the parking spot. "And also along that street, you'll find some shops."

"What are those white frames, Giuseppe?" I'm pointing to the dozens of thirty-footers marching down the wide expanse and around the castle. They're made in curlicue shapes forming a sort of paisley design.

"There's a big festival this weekend. A celebration of the patron saint, the *Festa della Fonte.* The castle is the center of activity in town. You'll find a lot going on all around it."

We're about to say *arrivederci* when John asks, "Is there a Piazza Garibaldi here? Or a street?"

Giuseppe gives a little laugh and shakes his head. "No. Not here."

Back in the apartment, we unpack our things and I sort through a pile of brochures and maps stored on the bookshelf. Amid the leaflets and flyers for Matera, Martina Franca, Lecce, Alberobello and several local spots, there's a large map of Conversano.

"This will be handy," I call to John who's across the room trying to figure out the TV. Opening the map on the kitchen table I smooth it wide and search for something familiar. I locate the road we drove in on and the divided one we walked up with our suitcases to get to the arch. "Okay, here's our street. I think the house is about here. This is the market street Giuseppe mentioned, and there's a piazza along it just a few blocks down. Maybe that's where the food shops are." I trace the street from our house back through where I think the archway is and along the broad pedestrian avenue next to the park we passed when we came in. "Here's the castle. Let's go up there later." There's another good-sized park opposite the castle and I squint closer to it. "Come over here! You won't believe this." John puts the clicker down and walks to the table.

"What?"

"Look at this. I guess Giuseppe doesn't know much about this town." My finger is resting beside the words in the center of the park: Villa Garibaldi.

"There's a *house* in that park?" he says.

"Must be. It says *Villa* Garibaldi. Let's walk there later and check it out."

In early evening we return to the street to join the *passeggiata* and explore. The broad pavement near the castle serves as the main thoroughfare and the whole town is turned out. A craft fair is set up under the white frames with stands offering ceramics, wooden bowls, and linens. At one, selling olives and nuts, we buy a small bag of roasted fava beans to nibble. The playful sound of a folksong draws us over to a small crowd. A man is blowing a mouthpiece into a short piano keyboard which he fingers accordion-style. His young son accompanies on the bongos. An odd combination but they're entertaining.

After a few minutes we follow other strollers around the castle to where the pavement widens even more, the main piazza. What must have been the old market street joins it here. Restaurant tables nudge the crowd on both its sides. Around us, people gather in small groups to exchange two-cheek *baci*, lovers slouch on each other's shoulders, and a shaggy mutt yips around his master's legs. A few people are drifting toward the entrance of the park we're looking for. Its iron gates are open and a broad marble stair leads between two substantial pillars. Closer, we can read the plaques on them.

VILLA GARIBALDI 1883

Up the stairs we see a long paved passageway extending to the opposite end of the park. Giant trees lining both sides have grown together, their branches forming a majestic, green cathedral. Planted gardens border each side of the shaded walkway. Benches rest along the outer edges of the park and, on one side, a children's merry-go-round and play area. The night air is cooler here. "What a pleasant space," I say to John. "It must be wonderful to come here on a hot afternoon. Do you think that's the villa over there?" On our left, under the hanging branches, we can see the first story and a half of what looks like a series of connected buildings. We follow along them until we reach a stairway that descends through a series of terraced gardens but we don't find any entrance. Nearby dozens of children's drawings are strung like laundry between the trees. Under spreading limbs, cut flowers cover a celebratory shrine set up for the festival of the saint.

"*Dov'e la villa?*" John asks a man on a bicycle. "*Villa Garibaldi?*" Where is it?

His reply, in Italian, "There's no villa. Just this park."

"Was it here before?" I ask.

He shakes his head. "No. There never was a house. It's always been just the park."

For a few minutes we gaze out beyond the shrine, past the city to where fruit and olive trees surround the homes. Then, hand in hand, we turn back under the arching arms of the arbor's long nave. "Garibaldi would have liked this," I say to John. "It's better than a statue, or even a piazza—and a lot more enjoyable."

"I think you're right. Of all the places we've seen, this feels like the most appropriate tribute. He didn't care about material things. He lived outdoors. So this is the perfect villa for him—the kind of monument that captures his spirit."

Exiting the green cathedral, we retrace our steps. Hunger is catching up with us. But as we round the bend in the wide walkway we hear music coming from an ornate white bandstand that's tucked near the side of the castle. Dozens of seats have been set up and almost all are full. From horns, woodwinds and timpani, the music beckons us. Puccini's "Tosca."

"Puccini's opera seems an odd selection for a brass band." John says.

"They're quite good though."

After a while we realize they're playing not just the arias but the entire score. Ducking into a couple of vacant seats near the front, we settle in to listen to our favorite opera, our growling stomachs forgotten.

That evening we scan our history books and search the Internet for some reference to Garibaldi being in Conversano. But we find none. Closing the iPad, John says, "Funny, isn't it. This place has no connection to Garibaldi, and yet, they created what might be the best memorial ever."

"E `aperto?" John asks from the doorway, his hat dribbling water onto his jacket. In the room beyond, more than a dozen puzzled faces stare back at us.

It's our second day in Conversano and Sunday. Still jet-lagged, we intended to sleep late. But here, it seems, the Church will have something to say about that. Around 10:30 the bells started. Bong, bing, bong, bong. Bing, bing, bong, bong. Loud. *Were they right next door?* I knew the tune as a Methodist hymn but probably it's a Catholic one here. Thankfully it stopped after three more tunes. But we were awake, so got up.

While John fiddled with the TV I poked around the kitchen to assess the cookware. Out in the street the noise started up again. This time a loudspeaker sounded like the priest was broadcasting mass all over the city. *"IN NOMINE PATRIS..."* If *they do this every Sunday it's sure to get people out of bed and into church.* I opened the shutters and leaned out over the tiny balcony. Below, women, children, men, old and young were walking up our street, and the one beyond, in the direction of the church. The loudspeaker droned on long after the street had emptied. *"AVE MARIA, GRATIA PLENA, DOMINUS TECUM..."* resounded through the apartment.

"I found some tea bags. Want a cup? I'm *cold.*" John agreed and I started a pot of water. We scrounged up some health bars and cookies I'd packed for the plane ride. By the time the water boiled, he'd also retrieved an apple from his backpack.

"*Buon appetito,*" he said offering an apple slice on the end of his pocketknife. I found a bit of honey in the cupboard and sweetened the tea. Warm slid down my throat to my stomach. Snuggled on the sofa we flipped through channels of bizarre Italian programming. John wanted a movie. For me, anything in English.

"Is that a band?" he said. The sound was coming quickly closer—thumping drums, horns, and clarinets.

I pulled the windows open again. "There's a crowd lined up along the street at the end of ours. Must be a procession." By the time I found my camera and figured out how to open the multi-locked door, it was gone. The street was empty. No sign of anyone in either direction. *Oh fiddlesticks.*

Back at the house I sorted through maps and city guides. Most of the places we want to see were here. I'm particularly curious about Alberobello. That's where the *trulli* are, and the only area of the country where they can be found. *Trulli*, the round, conical-topped stone structures are one of the things that most intrigue us. Made of local stone painted white, they look sort of like a Mongolian yurt. Their roofs, like inverted gray funnels, are made without mortar, a design origi-nated in the Middle Ages. Then, only completed buildings were taxed by the king, so the nobility forbade the peasants from using mortar for their roofs. When the tax collector was coming, the peasants would have to disassemble the roof so the building was "incomplete" and non-taxable. In recent years scores of English, Germans and other Europeans have converted *trulli* into "holiday houses" and shops. I'd looked into renting one for a few days, but they were pricey and mostly out in the countryside. Alberobello is home to an entire old town of *trulli*, all rejuvenated as restaurants, shops and homes and I can't wait to see it.

When we ventured out again it was two o'clock. A chilly drizzle had been falling and everyone had disappeared from the streets. Clothed in rain gear and clutching an umbrella from the house, we started looking for a place to eat. Beyond the archway we climbed the stairs to the pizzeria Giuseppe had recom-mended, but it was closed tight. Further up the hill we tried two other restau-rants, but they, too, were dark. Around the back of the castle, not even the coffee bar was open. *Surely those fancy places near the main piazza would be open.* But no.

"Maybe it's the *festa*," John said as we huddled under the umbrella in the drizzle. "Any excuse for a holiday."

"Great. We're starving in the country with the best food in the world." Cold rain on my thin slicker and damp socks, I was chilled through. Now the wind had picked up.

A few doors from the archway that led back to our rental house the white facade of a small restaurant had its glass doors thrown open. "Hey, that's open. Let's go," he said pulling my arm.

I held back. "I'm not sure. Look, there's just one long table and a bunch of people. Maybe a family? I think it's a private gathering." John was marching over, rain trickling from the brim of his safari hat. I hurried to catch up. "We shouldn't bother them. The doors are just open for air. Not for customers."

But he wasn't listening.

"*E` aperto?*" he says as we step up to the doorway. Is it open? Dripping and dowdy, our flapping umbrella gripped tight, we must look like hapless sailors washed ashore. Inside all the heads are turned to us. Most with startled looks. An old woman's face is frozen in a scowl.

"*E` aperto?*" His voice is a bit pleading. Far in the back a handsome thirty-something woman with a broad face whirls around. She's wearing a green plaid blouse and attractive round glasses.

"*Si!*" she calls to us. "*Una tavola la. Due sedie e una tovaglia. Laggiù.*" Her voice carries authority and several kids scurry to set a table for two with a white table-cloth across from the long one. She gestures for us to sit, then smiles. "*Benvenuto.*" Welcome.

"*Grazie. Grazie mille.*" Thank you so much. We hook our wet jackets over the ears of another chair.

She supervises the place settings and wine glasses then calls another younger man over. "This is my brother, Nicolo—Nik," she says in Italian. "He owns the restaurant. I'm Agata." Her large brown eyes beam confidence and warmth.

Nik gives his sister a knowing smile and turns to us. "This is a *latteria*, a restaurant where all the offerings are milk-based, sourced from local farms. But since it's a holiday the restaurant is closed and our family is having fish. If you don't mind eating what we're having, you're welcome to join us." I got stuck on *latteria*, but figured out most of what he said.

"*Certo*. We love fish," John replies in Italian putting on his best pilgrim's smile.

When Nik turns toward the kitchen I glance across the narrow room to the family table. About fifteen of them. The old woman must be the grandmother. Three thirty-something couples and a bunch of darling youngsters, mostly girls. Agata returns with wine glasses. *"Rosso o bianco?"*

"White first," John says and she nods approval.

"Andrea, porta una bottiglia." A fellow with mischievous eyes grabs a bottle from their table and heads over. He's tall for an Italian, over six feet with close-cropped hair that's beginning to retreat. "This is my husband, Andrea," Agata says, "and those girls are our daughters Rosie and Sadia. At the end that's my cousin and his family. And my mama." The old woman is still staring at us warily.

Nik brings our first course—oysters and a variety of clams, some not much bigger than a thumbtack. We slurp the larger ones from the shells. Their brine tastes like the sea. The tiny ones are hard to eat though and I ask Agata for some advice. "Stick your knife in and pull out the entire thing," she says, and it works. The pasta is a simple spaghetti with some shrimp, clams, a bit of calamari, a *langustino*, and a touch of parsley, smooth as butter, and probably laced with it. While we twirl our forks a conversation starts between our tables. Before long we're discussing the area, America, Garibaldi, and cherries.

"Conversano is famous for cherries and this is the season, "Agata tells us. "Why don't you come with Nik and me on Tuesday. We'll go cherry picking."

Yes!

Andrea and Agata pull chairs up to our table after the main course—breaded and baked fish light as air. She's an architect. He's an engineer and builder. They own a place in the hills where they've restored a series of *trulli* as a getaway. "Would you like to come up on Saturday? You can go for a swim and join us for a BBQ."

In the *trulli?* Truly? Oh, YES!

Nik sets a plate of soft cheeses on our table. "These are what I sell in my store. Also olive oil. It all comes from my farm." The cheese is unlike anything we've tasted. Mild and milky. My favorite is the *burattino*, a small ball of *buratta* with a silky, runny center that's scrumptious. The store isn't far and

Andrea, who speaks a little English, draws a map for me. He also sketches out the *trullo* construction and explains. "The round, stone base is topped with a two-layer roof made of carefully laid flat stones and no mortar. Air is trapped between the layers and keeps the room cool in summer and warm in winter." Ingenious.

Outside, an amplified, female voice chanting the Ave Maria is growing louder. "It's the final procession of the saint," Agata says as everyone moves out under the awning to watch. The rain has stopped and townspeople are walking by talking quietly. They're followed by white-robed priests and then four men in black suits and ties each carrying a tall pole topped with a massive sphere of white roses. Behind them, ten similarly clad men wearing white gloves, bear the saint's image on their shoulders like an Egyptian queen. *The fellow with a red-white-and-green sash across his chest must be the mayor.* And here's the band. Except they aren't playing, just strolling along, instruments in hand. More citizens, most wearing their best clothes—the line so long I can't see its end.

Curiosity satiated, our group wanders back in for *caffè*, but before long we hear more singing. This time it's not Ave Maria, but the happy sound of young girls coming from just beyond the doorway. I hurry outside where I find Agata's daughters watching two of their younger cousins giggle as they sing a rhyme. "Is it alright if I make a film?" I ask Agata, and she smiles and nods from the doorway. Clearly the center of attention now, the youngsters mug for me, clapping their hands to the tune over and over and over.

Agata laughs and calls gently to them, *"Arrivederci."* Slapping their hands a final time, the two of them wave at the camera. *"Arri-ve-DER-ci,"* they sing in unison. When I turn to the doorway again the old woman is watching, a tiny smile on her wrinkled face.

"There will be fireworks later," Andrea tells us once we've finished the last of the wine. "The best view is in front of Villa Garibaldi. You should go back there to see them." We make arrangements to meet Nik and Agata on Tuesday and get hugs from everyone in the room— even Mama. She feels tiny and frail in my arms, but her eyes twinkle and now a full smile spreads across her thin face.

Next to the castle wall, the bandstand is lit in glistening white lights and most of the dozens of chairs surrounding it are occupied for the concert. "That's 'Turandot.'" I say to John as we search for a seat just as they begin "Vincero."

People drift in and out of the seats and eventually we move on. There's still time before the fireworks will start, so we wander up the main street and around the corner where yellow light from the street lamps gives the buildings an eerie glow. The entrance to the town's church is in this small piazza. It's a plain building of square limestone, its only adornment the elaborate carved arch over the entrance guarded by a lion on each side. The door is open.

Inside it's a miniature of my beloved cathedral in Parma, but without the frescoes. These walls are the same plain, square stone as the exterior. Arches line the side aisles of the nave and above them, on the second story, light spills through the columned openings. The chancel too is bathed in flooded light but devoid of other decoration. The simplicity is beautiful. I've grown to love walking in old churches. I find peace in the serenity of their old walls and a feeling of connection with the centuries of people who have come here before. John has to remind me I'll miss the fireworks if we stay much longer.

At Villa Garibaldi, a crowd has gathered along the fence line. Fog is curling through the air. Under the arching arms of the tall trees, lighted decorations radiate halos of glowing green and yellow. Murmuring residents crowd the pathway in expectation. John inquires and learns there will be two test firings to determine if the fireworks display can be seen through the fog. Everyone is waiting, searching for where they'll be. POW! *Where did it came from?* No one is moving. A moment later—POW. This time I see a pale sparkle shower down behind the trees.

Turning to John, "I could barely make it out. I think it's too foggy. Could you see?"

"Not really. Let's head back." But before we can make much headway, POW , pop, pop, pop, POW , the show starts. It lasts about ten minutes and we strain to see much of it, then join the others walking homeward. Near the bandstand, the music is over and the band members are clustered around their instruments in lively conversation. In their gold-trimmed ivory jackets and black pants with the broad red side-stripe, they look quite handsome.

"*È stato un bel concerto,*" John says to a group of them. It was a beautiful concert.

"*Si. Mi piace molto,*" I add. Yes. I really liked it.

There's surprise on their pleased faces. *I'll bet they're thinking, where did these people come from?* America we say. *America!* One has a cousin in New York. Another hopes to go to visit next year. Their leader, a round-faced man in his fifties, worked in the States for a while.

"Did you come to Conversano for the festival?" someone asks in Italian.

"No, it was a surprise. We rented an apartment here for a month. On Via Jatta. We want to get to know the town."

More smiles and murmurs of appreciation. "So you'll get a chance to hear us play again," the leader says.

"We hope so," John says.

Cellphones appear and the photos start. One of the players steps back with mine to snap the group of us: a couple shy girls, several grinning fellows, and two delighted pilgrims from America.

I don't want to miss the band parade this morning, but, still travel weary, I can't wake up. When I hear them going by, I'm not dressed. Throwing clothes on I scramble out and hurry toward the castle. The band members are gathered under the trees across from the bandstand instruments propped nearby. The chairs from last night are gone.

"*La musica è finita?*" I ask a small group of men, disappointment in my voice.

"No, we will play later," one of them reassures me. He adds more, which I don't understand, but I thank him and promise to return. When John and I go out again an hour later we find them in the bandstand playing the score of "La Boheme." There's no one to hear except a handful of old men seated on the shaded benches. We sit with them for about half an hour then reluctantly move off on our errands.

After the ATM, market and pharmacy our destination is Masi, Nik's store for cheese and olive oil. It's tiny but has a considerable selection of cheeses. I purchase two fresh ones and a hunk of Parmigiano Reggiano plus chestnut honey, fresh-made orange spread and some crackers. We take a different path back and pass small shops I'm anxious to visit later.

"There don't seem to be many restaurants here," I say.

"Most everything seems to be just a bar or cafe serving pizza and *panini*."

"Maybe folks here don't eat out much."

In the evening I finally manage to catch the band playing as they pass near our street on their way to the castle. Afterwards, we return to Nik's restaurant for dinner where the frail-looking *nonna* now beckons us inside. We tell Nik to bring whatever he recommends which starts a procession of little dishes from his farms and vineyards. A plate of soft cheeses is the star, my favorite again is the *buratatini* with the soft, runny center.

Agata stops in later and reminds us we'll be going to the orchard Tuesday. I recall the video we saw this morning about the huge cherries that grow here. "This week is the *festa* of cherries," she says. "The piazza will be lined with all kinds of cherry products this week." *Another festival? Lucky us.* "I'll meet you at eleven," she says before we leave.

Walking slowly back to our little townhouse, I'm thinking about our rain-soaked meeting with Agata and her family. My husband always engages people. It might be chatting with a couple next to us at a bar, asking questions of the guard at a museum, or teasing the folks behind the counter in a restaurant or shop. He does it everywhere, but in Italy, he's always looking for a chance to practice his conversation skills. That means we have lots of encounters with locals—and we make Italian friends. I could never do this myself and I'm sure grateful he does.

Now back in our adopted "homeland" we've slipped easily into the relationship that characterized our year living here. No distractions or responsibilities to clutter up our day. Just cooperating on daily chores and challenges—helping and caring for each other. It's certainly easy to fall in love with the charm of

Italy. But I treasure this country so much because love and friendship are the center of our life here.

Seated on a bench beside the park on Tuesday morning, we're listening to the shouts and *whomps* of the boys playing soccer in the small amphitheater behind us. "Look up at the castle," I say, pointing to our right. "I guess even the count needs to do laundry." Next to the castle's squat turret is a three-story stone tower with a second-floor balcony. Strung from one side to the other are two rows of blouses, pants and baby dresses.

"No count any more. I'll bet they rent it out," John says.

Across from us is Nik's restaurant, named 219. "Agata said something about the name being related to the site. There's a plaque a few doors away. I'm going to see if I can read it." Luckily for me there's an English translation. The plaque marks the highest point in the area—two hundred nineteen feet above sea level. I've just returned to the bench and told John when Agata calls to us from the nearby parking area. We follow her to the car where Nik is behind the wheel.

Moments later we're heading out of town past rural residences where goats graze the yards. Agata points out the Church of St. Catherine, a tiny building in the shape of a cloverleaf. The top story, which supports a small bell tower, is octagonal. "This is the oldest building in the area," she tells us. "It marks the entrance to the town and was the first thing travelers would see when coming here."

Farther down the twisting road Nik indicates the field to our left. "*Terra Rosa*," he says. Red Earth. "Once there was a well here. The only one for the ancient city. Every day the women of the town would come here for their water, carrying it home on their heads. Back then the ruling count was—uh—a little crazy."

"More than a little," says his sister. "He made a decree that any time there was a marriage in the town, the bride would have to spend the first night in *his* bed, not her husband's."

"People here claim everyone is related," says Nik.

"Well, back to the count," Agata says. "He was known as a marksman—even though he was blind in one eye. He liked practicing his accuracy—on the women at the well. He'd sit in the castle up on the hill and take aim with his crossbow at the water jugs. It's a long shot. And he frequently missed." *Peasants and slaves, disposable by the powerful all over the world.* "That's why the ground was soaked in blood—Red Earth."

"That's a terrible story. What an awful guy," I say.

"He got his due," says Agata, a chuckle in her voice. "One young groom decided he wasn't going to cooperate. Sneaking up on the count from his blind side—he stabbed him."

"I can't imagine there was much mourning," John says.

"Probably dancing in the streets," says Nik.

We're passing ancient, gnarly olive trees, pruned back for decades to increase their production. Agata tells us some are centuries old. Scattered among the trees are swatches of orange poppies, heads wafting. At a break in the worn wooden fencing we turn into an orchard. The dirt road leads to a small, stone building. "This was our grandparents' home," says Agata. "My mother owns the property now, and gave each of us a portion. On the side there, the shed is where the animals lived, and just to the right of that is the outdoor kitchen." The tiny stone home has a heavy wooden door and only a couple small windows reminding me of America's pioneer cabins. *A hard life here.* "Come, we'll pick the cherries."

Trees are set about fifteen feet apart, the soil recently turned, so dry grasses poke through the soft loam. Like giant drops of blood, scarlet cherries dangle from leafy clusters. Bags in hand we spread out among the trees each pulling shiny fruit from the branches, sampling as we go. Only some of the trees bear cherries. Others nurture almonds and pears, both to mature later in summer. Our bags heavy, we've started back to the car when Agata gasps.

"*Guarda! Una vipera!*" The blue-black snake is curled next to a white-blooming weed.

"Is it dangerous?" John asks edging over.

"Poisonous," she says, and he backs away.

We all move closer—but not too close—to take a look. The viper is several feet long but appears content to warm itself in the sun. *I'm certainly glad we found it here and we didn't traipse on it during the picking. Another peril of rural life.*

At the end of the dirt road, before we pull out onto the main one, John asks Nik to stop.

"My father was a stonemason," he says. "That wall is fabulous." Along the opposite side of the road it stands twelve feet high, the top quarter overhanging a few inches like a crown moulding. The stones are perfectly flat on the exterior but assembled like a crazy quilt from various shapes and sizes in shades of white, gray, rust and dusty orange. Near the corner it rises another two feet and we can glimpse the thickness—a couple feet. We get out to examine it and snap a photo. "See," John says. "there's no mortar. Only a master can build something that tall and long without mortar. They fill the space between the two walls with rubble, then cap it with concrete to keep the rain from washing through."

Running my hand over the almost-smooth surface I say. "I never get over the craftsmanship that goes into everything here. I wonder how long it took to build this." No one has a guess.

Back in the car once more, Nik drives back into town. Before he drops us off where we met, Agata leans toward the back seat. "I can show you around the old part of the city on Thursday if you like." We give each other a look. Yes! "I'll meet you at eleven in the same place."

That evening I spread out the Conversano map and we try unsuccessfully to follow the path to the family orchard. Munching enormous, sweet cherries we abandon the map for reading on the sofa. I look up from my novel a short while later, "Nik reminded us of next week's cherry festival up by the castle, so we ought to go."

"If the festival cherries are half as good as these we definitely have to. These will be gone long before that." He grabs another handful.

"Never as sweet as the ones you pick yourself." I slap his hand from the bowl. "You can't have *all* of them. *Che fortunata,*" I say as we finish the bowl. How fortunate. "Today we picked cherries and Saturday we'll visit a *trullo*. Not four days in this town and we found more than an open restaurant. Once again, we've been adopted."

SUNDAY IN THE PARK WITH NANCY

Do not go gentle into that good night,
Old age should burn and rave at close of day;
Rage, rage against the dying of the light.

DYLAN THOMAS

CONVERSANO, ITALY

Why can't I simply enjoy the moment? Here I am, in Italy, with Nancy. It's a beautiful spring day. Sunday. The lovely town of Conversano, in Puglia. A picnic in tree lined Villa Garibaldi. Just the two of us. On a park bench. Our lunch—bread, Felino salami, Parmigiano and a bottle of Primitivo red—sits between us on a copy of today's *Gazzetta del Mezzogiorno*. Birds are singing. Flowers are in bloom. Folks are walking by chatting, smiling, laughing.

I'm ranting.

It's a fact. The USA is the only advanced country without a true national health system. If national health is so bad, why do Italians outlive us by two-and-a-half years? They also have a far lower incidence of obesity and diabetes. Probably has something to do with breastfeeding. Women here breastfeed in public. Get it? Diabetes. Obesity. Lifespan? Interesting, eh?

Down the path comes a family on bikes. Cute kids. Oh, no. The mom is smoking! That doesn't fit the picture.

Ah, this is more like it. A tall, thin gentleman suited in dark blue, topped with a black homburg. Perfect. And, these two pretty teenage girls dressed in real dresses, walking hand in hand. Very Italian. Excellent. Oh, and this. Yes, yes. A striking middle-aged lady arrayed in flowing whites saying 'No, No' to convention by insouciantly opting to use a large black golf umbrella as a parasol. Nice touch. I love it.

What the— Would you look at this! Two tattooed string beans with blue Mohawks. Blue Mohawks with orange tips! Wrong! Wrong! Wrong! I ask for Seurat and they give me surreal. Wrong!

Nancy's approving laugh is all the permission I need to reprise my rant.

So, OK, everybody knows about the beneficial effects of red wine. The Italians certainly have us beat there. But listen to this. Yesterday, I read in the *New York Times* about a Harvard study that proved lonely people die younger. No wonder Italians outlive us. Hell, it's not unusual for three, even four generations, to be living in the same house. There are four generations at my cousin Claudia's. The place is a virtual commune. Anyway, here, fewer women work outside the home. It's got to be easier to breastfeed if you're not working. No?

Don't get me wrong. I am not obsessing about breasts. The only points I'm contemplating are these: We may have the best doctors in the world, but our healthcare system sucks. As a percent of GNP, we Americans spend three times as much on healthcare as do Italians; yet our outcomes— things like life spans, infant mortality rates, diabetes, and deaths by infections—are not nearly as good. It makes no sense. Why doesn't the government simply tell us the way it is?

My little fill-in-the-blank quiz would drive any ordinary woman crazy, but Nancy simply smiles, sips the Primitivo, pretends to listen, strokes my hand.

Her touch puts me into high gear.

OK. OK. Here it is. My fellow Americans, based on scientific evidence gathered by our crack research team in Italy, effective immediately all nursing women will be shipped to communes where they will receive full pay…and… and…a daily ration of red wine…and cigarettes too…if they want them… and salami…all the salami they can eat. Thank you for your cooperation. May God bless you and your families and may God bless the United States of America.

Nancy laughs. I smile. We hold hands. We're in the moment.

Now, paint the picture.

OF PATRIOTS AND HEROES

Show me a hero and I'll show you a tragedy.

F. SCOTT FITZGERALD

CONVERSANO, ITALY

It's our second week in Conversano. John, the early riser, always makes our coffee. The Italian espresso pot is missing the rubber washer between the top and bottom halves. The first time he used it, coffee and grinds bubbled all over the stove, so he'll be improvising. I've seen him do it many times. He folds a paper towel into a filter and puts it inside a large funnel that he places over a small pot. Scooping coffee into the towel, he pours boiling water over it, waiting while it drains before adding more. The aroma drifts up the stair to the bedroom.

I open the polished wood shutter and the glass door behind. Light, and the cool morning spill into the bedroom. From the narrow street below I hear quiet voices of parents walking their youngsters to school and the clip clip of heels on the timeworn cobblestones. After making our bed I pad downstairs for my cup and open the three tall shutters there. *I like this apartment.* The outer walls are ancient stone; the interior plaster ones painted white. A modern concrete stair, which turns at the base, hangs on the rear wall. Tucked under it are a TV and comfy sofa. The typical Italian one-wall kitchen lies across the room beyond a glass table and four bright-orange modern chairs. The table's covered now with brochures, our backpacks, bags of bread and biscotti, and a bowl holding cherries, lemons, an eggplant, my camera and tiny travel purse.

John hands me a cup of milk and *caffè*. "Don't dally around this morning. We're meeting Agata at ten."

"Wasn't it nice of her to offer to show us around town?" I sip carefully hoping my brew isn't too hot. After our trip to the orchard she had suggested a tour of the old city.

"It's going to be interesting to hear what an architect has to say." He opens a white paper bag and removes a thick biscotto for himself and one for me, dunking his deep in his cup before taking a bite. "Maybe this afternoon we can take a drive."

"Sure, we'll see what's close by to explore."

Two hours later, we descend the steep, narrow stone steps from the living area to the front door, slide the heavy latch and turn the ancient key in its lock to open. The door locks automatically, so from the top of the steps outside, John holds the key up for me to see, then pockets it and pulls the door tight. *Click* goes the battered iron lock. Across the street a large ground level door is open. Inside sits a wizened little man in his wheelchair, a shawl draped over his jacket. His left leg is missing and he's watching us. As we approach he gives us a smile.

"*Ciao,*" I call to him.

"*Buongiorno signore,*" says John as we pass.

He gives us a nod and little wave with his weak reply. "*Buongiorno.*"

Agata joins us at the usual spot in front of Nik's and the three of us walk back toward the stone archway John and I just passed through. Before reaching it we turn up a stone stair making a left at the top into an old monastery.

Agata says, "It was founded in the sixth century by Benedictines and was once the most important monastery in Puglia. Sometime in the 13th century the Pope gave it to the Cistercian nuns. They were an extraordinary group. Wealthy families would send their first-born daughter to enter this monastery." Her eyes twinkle and there's a smile in her voice as she adds, "The sisters here wore a mitre, like the ones the bishops wear today—the only women ever allowed to

wear those religious trappings. The bell tower you see above the walls is supposed to symbolize the superiority of the nuns over the local bishop." *Our
architect is a feminist.*

For the next hour we meander the old town. Everything is made of stone.
Narrow passageways are paved with smooth rectangular cobblestone often set in
a diagonal. More rectangular stonework forms the base of buildings up to chair
rail height, smaller stones above. Sometimes a row of a different size delineates
where a second story starts. Some of the doorways have Gothic arches like those
in a church and occasionally a windowed passageway spans across the narrow
street connecting buildings on both sides. Agata points out buildings she and
Andrea renovated, and one that's their current project. We stop into the school
she attended as a youngster and visit its Baroque chapel. Exiting the school, we
give Agata a hug and thank her for our tour.

After lunch we drive to nearby Rutigliano, a place I had considered as our
base. Small factories and enterprises line the approaching roads. A disappoint-
ing town mostly populated with nondescript beige apartment buildings, it feels
too commercial. Thankfully, Conversano's castle caught my imagination.

"I'm happy we decided to find a place in the old city," I say to John when
we return to Conversano. "It's such a beautiful little town and now I appreci-
ate it even more." Residents are out on the narrow streets now, on their way to
pick up dinner at a rotisserie or sweets at the bakery. "We wouldn't have the
same experience if we were in some modern apartment building. This feels like
authentic Italian living."

Across from our entry, the big doorway is closed; the little man in the
wheelchair must have gone inside. "Tomorrow, let's go to Alberobello," John
says as he clicks the lock.

The next morning is overcast and even inside it's chilly. Doesn't bode well for
our Alberobello exploration. "This is *May* in *southern* Italy," I say pulling on
my thin rain jacket, the warmest thing I've got with me. "I didn't expect to be

---

freezing." John shrugs, buttons a long sleeve shirt over his t-shirt and slips into his safari jacket.

"Put a hat on," he says punching his red Phillies cap. "Got the map?"

Outside, we wave to the little man in the wheelchair as we pass by. *Ciao, ciao,* and head to the car.

When we reach Alberobello about a half hour later the narrow streets are jammed with cars. Once we locate a parking spot on a residential street I take a photo of the shop on the corner so we'll be able to find our way back. Following signs for the Trulli District we find ourselves on Corso Vittorio Emmanuel. The street is named for the first king of the unified Italy. The man Garibaldi met in Teano to hand over the Kingdom of Two Sicilies and unify the country.

"Maybe there's a Garibaldi statue along here," John says. But we don't see one and I'm not interested in searching right now. I'm *cold.*

"Looks like a big piazza up ahead. And a market! Hurray. Maybe I can find a jacket."

"Over here," John calls a few minutes later. He's standing by a tent filled with sweatshirts. "Pick one of these." Most are too big, or ugly, but I find one that fits. Dark blue with 72 on the sleeve and a patch over the breast that reads *New York Royal Canadian Yachting and Sailing.* Very Italian. Sold! I zip it up and slip my rain jacket back on as John says, "That's so like them—mashing New York and Canada into a single logo. Close, but not right."

Not far beyond the last vendor stand we come to a long staircase leading to the street below. Both of us stop to take in the sight on the opposite hillside. "Amazing. The whole hill is covered with them," John says. Whitewashed buildings scrunch together up the twisting streets, their roofs, like upside-down funnels, made of gray stone. An entire village of trulli: It looks like a Conehead convention.

I remember the guidebook I read last night. Building started over a thousand years ago when the first count of Conversano got this land as a reward for his service in the Crusades and started moving peasants here. That story about making mortarless roofs to avoid taxation? It's true—at least once—when the King of Naples sent his tax collectors to the village. By the end of the 18th century *trulli* building had pretty much stopped. Now this is a UNESCO site.

I flip the hood of my jacket up. "Nothing like it anywhere else. Come on. Looks like the rain could start again any minute."

Under darkening skies, we hurry down the stair, across the wide piazza and choose what appears to be the main street. The walk up is Disney-charming. Paved with stone and occasional low steps the slope is an easy walk. *All the better for visiting tourists.* Lining both sides are shops offering tea towels, aprons, tablecloths, and pot holders decorated with a border of *trulli* in various colors. The wares are displayed on wooden shelves outside the simple arched entrance, enticing you inside. Other shops offer decorated pottery or miniature *trulli*, the perfect size for a curio cabinet. Flowering vines creep up from the pavement and across many of the doorways. We poke into shops and glance inside restaurants and homes for the next couple hours. Many of these *trulli* have been "modernized" with drop ceilings, overhead lighting, and other attachments that have altered the interior. It's kind of a shame. *People have to live in a place, but the town's economy depends on tourism. You'd think the owners would be more careful to show the historic setting. I guess UNESCO doesn't look beyond the door.*

On our way back to the car we pass through the piazza where I bought my sweatshirt. The market tents are gone now and we can see what it looks like. Just beyond a treed seating area the piazza opens wide as we approach Via Vittorio Emmanuel.

"Honey, look over there!" I say pointing to the opposite side. "There's the Garibaldi tribute." It's a government building of some sort with flags of Italy, the commune, and the EU over the main entrance and window boxes on the balconies filled with red geraniums. Flanking columns on either side of the entrance, two huge stone plaques are set into the wall. In Italian they read:

To Victor Emmanuel
Founder of the United Italy
1885

To Giuseppe Garibaldi
Avenger of Liberty
1885

"I'm not surprised to find a tribute to the two of them on a government build-ing," John says. "But I doubt it reflects the feelings of the residents. We probably won't see grand statues here in the south. After all these were the conquered lands Garibaldi handed to the monarch. I don't think either is well loved here."

"It's a nice tribute though," I say. "Equal billing with the king."

On Friday morning I tackle the laundry. Washing machines are never intuitive and Italian machines have a mind of their own. When Giuseppe came to fix the TV I'd asked him to show me how this one works. After fiddling with the dials for a few minutes he took out his phone—and called his mother. Acting as translator, he relayed her instructions. Now I know how it works. But the other day when I washed, it went through the entire cycle without getting the clothes wet. Today success is mine.

Arms piled with damp garments I climb the two flights to the narrow ter-race where the hanging racks are. On the patio across the street a stocky, gray-haired woman in a loose-fitting dress is taking in her wash. She gives me a smile and nod. I pull out a sheet and let it gently drop over the front of the building, attaching it to one of the three lines stretched for that purpose. As I'm shak-ing out the second, I hear the woman calling in Italian. "Are you renting that house?"

"*Sì.*" In my best Italian I add, "We're staying in Conversano for a month."

She looks surprised. "A month? In Conversano?"

Why are locals always surprised we want to spend time in their area? "It's a beautiful town. I didn't know much about it when I rented this place, but we're so happy we chose it. We'll visit other places, but this will be our base. We like the house and have made some friends in town." She looks puzzled. *Did I say something wrong?*

"My husband is not well," she says, her tone agitated. "It's very difficult for me. He can't get around at all and so I have to do everything." Pulling men's shirts and boxers from the line as she speaks, she gives them a rough fold and piles them into a plastic basket. "The only time he goes out is to the doctor. He just sits. He eats. He sleeps. Me, I do everything. He doesn't even talk much." She says a lot more, but it's pretty fast and I have a hard time following so I just nod and look sympathetic. I catch a bit about their children coming sometimes. Maybe he served in a war? Or a service organization? Can't figure it out. She's on a little rant.

"I'm sorry for your troubles," I say hanging the final shirt. "I hope your husband is better soon." Gathering my basket up I give her a wave. "*Ciao, signora.*"

I'm just getting to the bottom of the stairs in the living room when John says, "Agata called. She and Andrea invited us to go to an *agritourismo* dinner tonight with some of their friends. Then we'll go to the *trulli* on Sunday morning."

"I swear Agata is set on making sure we don't miss a thing." I set my laundry basket on top of the washer and turn back into the living room. "I met the woman across the street. She was taking her laundry in and said hello. She said a lot more too. I think she's pretty stressed out. Her husband is ill. He must be the little man in the wheelchair we see in the mornings."

"Probably. It's too bad. He looks like a nice old fellow."

"Well, she went on and on about how much work he's making for her."

"Just like our house," he says with a laugh. "You do all the work." It's one of his favorite lines.

"Right. So give me a hand with lunch will you."

"Sure." He heads for the refrigerator. "You make the panini and I'll open the wine."

The next morning, as I'm making the bed, clamorous voices rise from the street. Opening the shuttered window, I see three men struggling to carry the old man from across the way up the stairs to the home's entrance. A middle-aged woman follows them slowly from behind and the lady from the rooftop seems to be issuing instructions at the door. Their burden is frail, but the stairs are narrow and steep and the men have difficulty. Gently, they maneuver him through the door and into the house. I close the window, gather our backpacks and join John downstairs.

Andrea picks us up after breakfast and we drive south past Noci and on to their summer home in the hills. "We're having a BBQ today," he says. "A lot of our friends are coming. And their kids too. Tonight you'll sleep in the *trullo*."

On the narrow roads outside the towns we pass olive groves, grape arbors, and cherry orchards. *Trulli* buildings, some crumbling, others converted for modern use grow more numerous as we travel south.

"That's a pretty one," I say as we pass a modernized version.

"Agata wouldn't like it," Andrea says shaking his head. "She only does *authentic* buildings. That one added a modern front and destroyed its original shape. Many of the old ones were once used for commercial purposes—grain storage for example. So, some of them were expanded into larger spaces for modern business use. But many home conversions retain little of the original except the characteristic roof."

"That's too bad," John says. "I guess not everyone appreciates the authenticity."

"I admire what you and Agata do—restoring old buildings," I say. "Honoring the past isn't easy. But it's good to celebrate what came before—what brought us to where we are now."

Andrea turns toward us with a grin. "You know, if it weren't for the rain we would never have met. We're *simpatico*, all of us, even through the language barrier." It's true, I feel completely at ease with these warm folks, as if we shared a great grandmother. A moment later, Andrea's husky baritone belts out a familiar tune. "*A-rri-vider-ci trulli...*"

Laughing, we join in, "Goodbye, goodbye, goodbye..."

At their property we pull into the long dirt drive just ahead of Agata and the girls. Rosie and Sadia pile out of the car and start carrying things into a low stone building as their mother explains it to us. "We built this with the stone from the old walls that lined the property. It's more spacious than the *trulli* with plenty of room for entertaining and a real kitchen."

As we're unloading our things two more cars pull into the drive. The exiting women carry covered platters and foil-wrapped dishes into the house. John takes in the several bottles of wine we brought. The great room is all white—floor, walls, slip-covered furnishings, accents, soft cotton drapes, even the chandeliers. Stylish and comfortable. Looping across the fireplace is a remnant of Christmas pine. A long white Parson's table seats ten and another one seating six is draped with a white cloth. At the far end of the room, behind a chest-high wall, is a galley kitchen. Baskets and platters are stored in shelves and niches on its back wall.

More people are arriving with food that quickly fills the kitchen counters and the long table. While the women are busy in the kitchen Andrea shows us behind the curtained doorway to where there are a couple bedrooms and a bath. "We stay here when it's too cold to use the *trulli,*" he says. "Or when it's rented. You two will stay there tonight. Get your things and I'll unlock it."

Five of the conical-topped buildings huddle in a row. Builders' emblems cap four of them. On the fifth and largest one at the end, missing stones form a ladder up the roofline to its peak.

"It'll be a bit chilly," Andrea says as he unlocks the door. "We haven't been here for a few months. I'll turn the heater on. There are plenty of blankets, though, if you're cold tonight."

We step across the two-foot-deep threshold and duck through the door. An all white interior enfolds us. Curved iron legs protrude under the king-sized bed which is covered with a white, scalloped-edge quilt and white and beige pillows. Simple furnishings, some painted white others patinated antiques. A stone floor. A few hooks for clothing. Behind the bed, a draped linen cloth serves as headboard.

Andrea leads us down four stairs and into a connecting hallway that goes to another bedroom and the bath. Along the hallway a tree branch hangs on the wall and four small birdhouses, woven from thin offshoots, dangle from it on cords.

"This is the girls' room when we stay here. It used to house the animals and was already attached to the old *trullo.* Part of the original use, so we converted it." Twin beds, white bureau, and white linen curtains. Light pours in from the standard-size doorway that was once the entrance to the stable. Around the corner, there's a good-sized shower, marble-topped sink with a few blue-and-white tiles for backsplash, a washing machine, bidet and toilet—the kind you'd find in an old Victorian with water housed in a wooden box mounted high on the wall and a long pull chain to flush.

The opposite end of the hallway leads to a small room with a wood-burning fireplace. "This was the original kitchen," Andrea says. "Now it's just a sitting area." He ducks through the opposite doorway. "This is the main room now."

It's a good-sized space with an alcove jutting from the rear where twin beds do double duty as sofas. A square table, covered with a beige cloth, and white chairs stand in the center of the room, and along the side a sink and small cook-top. Next to the exterior door a refrigerator and small sofa hug the curved wall.

"It's absolutely charming," I say. "Just adorable. I can see why people like staying in these."

We settle ourselves into the bedroom and then return outside. The whole gang is here now, about twenty adults all gathered under the pergola that covers the patio in front of the *trulli* with fig branches and grapevines. The men surround a long table, the women sit on benches nearby. *Oh, good. Carmella and Gabriella, the English-speaking women I met last night, are here.* Out in the yard, the kids are kicking a soccer ball near the pool. Food appears course after course— roasted vegetables, salads, plates of sliced meats. The women don't drink much, but the men are making up for us, arguing and laughing around their table. More food; baked pasta, chicken, and lasagna, a sweet cake and bowls of fruit.

Gabriella and Carmella tune me into the girls' conversation. They laugh over family stories and silly romantic ideas. Girl talk. When discussion turns to their book club. I tell them about the one we've had for over twenty years.

"Have you read *Gattopardo?*" someone asks me.

In English it's *The Leopard.* Probably the most famous book in Italy after Dante's *Inferno.* "Yes, we read it a couple years ago. John read it both in English and Italian. It really gives you an idea of what the aftermath of Garibaldi's Unification was like for the people of Sicily. We watched the movie, too, when we lived in Parma." Before I can ask what the group thought of the portrayal of post-unification Sicily, the conversation has veered to popular films.

Around three o'clock we move inside, the women around the long dining table, the men playing cards at the small one. Some of the kids flop on the sofas to thumb their cellphones. A large bowl of potato chips and a single bottle of Coke sit on the table; the kids help themselves from time to time. We drink water from small plastic cups, the size you get at the dentist office for swishing, and they're never filled to the top. Both last night and today, food was consumed in small quantities, over an extended time. What's savored around this table is camaraderie.

Late in the evening, when everyone has departed, we sit with Agata and Andrea on the patio watching a crescent moon and fading sunset behind the *trulli* before we turn in for the night. Snuggled under two blankets, we sleep well. The next day Agata drops us back in Conversano with recommendations from them for towns to visit; Martina Franca, Ostuni, Locorotundo, Trani, Matera's Sassi caves—overnight for the lights— Lecce, also for an overnight, and Polignano a Mare.

The dining table in our Conversano living area is littered with maps, brochures from towns in Puglia, an open bag of my favorite fennel-laced hard crackers, John's pen knife, a bowl containing oranges, pears, tomatoes and car keys, a pocket Italian dictionary, a bag of roasted chickpeas, and the remains of our snack of *salumi* and Parmigiano. I stare into the small refrigerator. Liters of water, tiny bottles of my favorite Crodini soda, and half-empty bottle of white. Mushrooms, butter, pancetta, white-wrapped cheeses, two fennel bulbs, milk, cream, eggs, the few remaining marinated anchovies, and half of the panino I didn't finish for lunch yesterday.

"I think we should go out for dinner. Or else walk to the little market." I glance at the wall clock. "It's not too late to pick up something. What do you say?"

John is engrossed in an Italian novel, our larger dictionary laid across his thigh. He swipes his glasses off, sticks his chin out and purses his lips in a characteristic squinty face, then nods agreement. "I'll take you out. How about we go back to the little square where they have the covered pergolas?"

"*Buon idea.* There are a couple places around the piazza we could try."

Our course follows the ancient cobble-stoned streets that weave up and down, past a few shuttered shops and homes where we hear voices and the clatter of dishes coming from curtained doorways. Descending a slope into the small piazza, we pass the open door of a restaurant kitchen where a worker is forming pizza dough into balls. The piazza is deserted except for people on their way to somewhere else. Along the perimeter we step around several grizzled old men planted in plastic chairs outside what appears to be a local club. Through the open doorway we see others gathered around tables playing cards.

"How about we sit over there?" John signals the heavy wooden tables under a grapevine arbor and we find a seat. Momentarily a young woman appears. *"Mi dispiace che non siamo aperti ora."* Not open yet. Seven o'clock she adds. It's five-thirty now. Before we can reconsider, she says, *"Volete una birra?"* Would we like beer? You bet. She returns with a cloth to clean the table, then a few minutes later with two mugs. Relaxing, shaded from the late afternoon sun, we watch the few people starting to appear around the square and listen to the baritone mumble of old men gathered outside a building next to the restaurant. Occasionally it's punctuated by an assertive tenor voice making his *punto*.

Over the serving window of the restaurant is the name: *Amici Miei*, My Friends. "What does that word mean? *Norcieria*." John's Italian is so much better than mine, his vocabulary especially good.

"I don't know. It's some kind of specialty, but not one I've heard. We'll have to look it up."

There's another sign over the doorway of the place next door where the old men are. An association—and something about freedom. John motions to the young woman who gave us the beer and asks about it.

"It's a place for veterans," she says. "That sign? It says Association for the Release of POWs."

We ponder what POWs it's referring to as we watch the two young women bustling in and out of the restaurant. Each is slender and in her twenties with long hair, t-shirts and jeans. Our *cameriera* is a light brunette, her co-worker darker. They wash all the heavy tables and wipe down the chairs. Next, one mops the floor inside while the other polishes the windows and menu glass. A third young woman has arrived and we see her through the open serving window, her knife chop-chopping a rapid beat. At the familiar sound of metal scraping pavement I search the piazza for skateboarders—but there are none. Instead, it's the tiny waitress muscling a heavy metal barrel into place. The other pulls out a short ladder and the two of them hang a couple dozen candles in glass globes from the arbor branches. Not long afterwards they emerge from the side of the building now wearing pressed skirts and pretty blouses, their hair pinned up, ready for an evening waiting tables.

"Can you imagine a waitress in America doing all that?" I say.

John watches the girls set out tableware. "And I'll bet it's not even their place."

The square is coming to life now. People drifting into the nearby pizzeria and bar. At around 7:15 a short stocky fellow in his thirties with a dark mustache and clipped goatee crosses the *piazza* and enters the restaurant.

"Bet that's the owner," John says. A few minutes later the young woman who brought us beer returns to our table with menus and John asks her about him.

"*Si, il padrone.*" She leaves us to peruse the menu and a few minutes later the owner strolls up to our table.

"*Buona sera,*" he says. Playful, dark eyes below heavy brows. With that neat-trimmed beard he reminds me of Shakespeare's Puck. We introduce ourselves in Italian and tell him about our stay in Conversano. His name is Massimo.

"I want to learn English," he says during our chat. "Also to visit America." Our conversation covers the usual litany of great cities, Italian and stateside. Massimo laughs when John uses a few Sicilian words. "My wife is Sicilian," he says, "so I understand their dialect."

"That's what I heard at home," says my husband. "My Sicilian is better than my Italian."

"What is a *norcieria?*" I ask when there's a lull between them.

"I serve pork products from Norcia, a town about five hundred kilometers north. I think they're the best. We have quite a few of Norcia's specialties on the menu." From his recommendations we choose our supper. As we're waiting for our dinner our waitress brings a plate filled with chunks of grilled meat.

"*Mortadella di cinghiale,*" she says. Mortadella made from wild boar. "You have to try it. Compliments of Massimo."

This thick version of the familiar Italian product is especially tasty and we agree grilling enhances the flavor. "I'll have to try this back home. It won't be *cinghiale*, but thick-cut mortadella would be almost as good."

Next door, the old vets are still engaged in a lively conversation. When we finish our meal, John pushes his chair back. "Let's go talk with them."

There he goes again engaging people. Our time in Italy is richer for it. But I know it'll be too hard for me to understand the gravelly voices and I think the old fellows will be more receptive to a man. "You go. I'll wait here."

He approaches the group of five clustered at the doorway. Heads nod, some welcoming laughs. A few minutes later they call out another. He's slender but not frail with alert eyes and leans forward, turning his head when others speak. The other men are deferential. Even in an ordinary blue-and-white plaid shirt, blue vest and dark pants, his affect is elegant, almost patrician. I notice he gestures only with his right hand and wonder if the other is injured, or missing. He keeps his left arm tucked behind his back. In the ensuing conversation he's the primary speaker. After several minutes they all go inside.

John returns to our table eventually. "So tell me about it," I say.

"You wouldn't believe it, but that fellow is ninety-two. Giuseppe Battista is his name and he fought with the *Partigiani* against the Germans at Monte Cassino. Remember that battle? How the Allies bombed the monastery where the Germans were dug in? And then it was even worse rooting them out? It was one of the Allies' bloodiest victories."

"Uh huh, I remember."

"When we went inside he showed me a photo of his *Partigiani* group, with him as a young freedom fighter."

"Sorry I didn't see that. Must have made him proud to show you." Monuments to the *Partigiani* are all over Italy. I'm thinking of the one in Parma's Parco Pace, the Peace Park, where there was always a wreath in the grassy area at its base and a crowd sitting on the low wall that surrounds it. "The *partigiani* were kind of like Garibaldi's troops, right? Fighting to run off the foreigners and give Italy back to the Italians."

"Well sort of. World War II was a little different though. Old Giuseppe was lamenting that their group—the World War II vets—is getting smaller and over the years it's been supplemented with many others. Now the role of the elder ones is almost lost. Once they were working to gain freedom, and then recognition, for their POW comrades. Now, their mission's nearly disappeared and it's become just a place for any old men to gather, talk and play cards."

Like Garibaldi before them, once the fight was over, they were relegated to their wheelchairs. "That's sad, especially for someone like him. He had a gravitas I could feel just looking."

"Strong and plain-speaking. He reminded me a little of Jacques Cousteau."

While we're talking the little group outside the Association is breaking up. Giuseppe Battista emerges from the building, rolls his bicycle from the rack, and slowly pedals away.

"I should have bought them all a beer," John says watching him disappear. "Maybe we'll see him again next time."

The weather has finally warmed so today we'll drive to Poglinano a Mare to visit the beach. On our way to the car in the morning, we see the little man is back inside the doorway. *I wonder what he's waiting for?* His face brightens when he sees us and he straightens up a bit when he waves. "*Buongiorno,*" his weak voice calls. Anxious to get on the road, we return his wave, smile—*Ciao. Ciao.*—and head up the street.

Half an hour later we've parked near the center of the beach town. On our left as we stroll toward the gated entrance to the center, a wrought-iron enclosed memorial bisects the street. "That statue looks like a World War One soldier," I say. The larger-than-life granite figure clutches his rifle while looking over his shoulder. Below him, in relief, a frieze of soldiers rushes forward, weapons in hand, while several of their comrades sprawl on the ground. A wreath is propped at the monument's base between two huge bowls of red geraniums.

"Well, look at this," John says when we come closer. The inscription reads

From Polignano and Her Sons Living in America to the Fallen.
1924

And her sons living in America? John answers my unspoken question. "I imagine by then an awful lot of young men had emigrated to the States, but still had family back here. Italians and Americans—from the same extended families— would both have died in battle."

"It's an unusual inscription. A reminder of the role Italian immigrants played in our American history."

Nearby we descend a long path to the beach—its aqua water so beautiful to look at—but the shore is covered in grapefruit-sized rocks. Walking to the water we both struggle to keep from turning an ankle, but the locals are unfazed, sunning themselves on towels thrown across the bumpy terrain. When we arrive back on the cliffside overlooking the pristine sea we discover another enormous statue. This one in bronze. Arms spread wide, head thrown back, suit jacket hanging free and scarf knotted neatly beneath his open shirt, he appears to be singing. "Volare" it's called. Polignano native Dominico Moldugnio popularized this Italian classic—one of the most famous Italian songs ever. The Dean Martin version became an America standard. *Volare*, to fly. On this sunny afternoon, in this whitewashed, seaside town, on an adventure with the man I love, I feel it too. I spread my arms, tilt my face up. Your love is giving me wings.

Our last weekend in Conversano, Agata and Andrea have invited us back to the *trulli*. Their friend Rosanna, who we met briefly last weekend, wants to make a Sicilian dinner for us. We drive there with Andrea again and meet the rest of the family at the house. Rosanna and husband Francesco pull up a half hour later with several foil-wrapped packages, then the men disappear into town for the barbecue supplies. They return with a dozen football-sized octopi they will cook on the wood-fired grill. I'm not sure where I acquired my taste for octopus—certainly not in my Scotch-Irish home. Grilled octopus is now one of my favorite preparations, so I leave the others and go outside to see how it's done. As I get closer, the smoky wood aroma tempts me closer. Suspended over the coals in grill baskets, a dozen flattened octopi are sizzling as they darken.

Once they're done, Andrea grabs each one with tongs and bathes it in olive oil before bringing them all inside. The table is laid with calamari "cooked" in lemon juice, tomato-topped focaccia sprinkled with cheese, and raw carrot sticks. We each get an octopus and I'm anxious to cut into mine. Black, crispy nodules along the legs retain the charcoal aroma. My knife easily slices through the tender flesh, its texture similar to a mushroom and smoky on the tongue.

Next comes a casserole of *anelli*, a tiny donut-shaped pasta, cooked in tomato sauce and topped with slices of *caciacavelli* cheese and fried eggplant. For dessert there's a cake made with watermelon and a few scattered chocolate bits—a fruit-flavored sponge that practically dissolves in my mouth. After the plates are cleared the kids go outside and the rest of us settle around the table sipping bottled water or wine. Our conversation drifts from Francesco's reports of local news, to pasta shapes from Sicily and Puglia, to Andrea's garden, to our Conversano rental home.

"Matera certainly was an experience," John says when Agata asks about our explorations of the past week. "It's hard to grasp how people lived in those caves until the fifties. Or why."

"They had no choice. Poor is poor," says Francesco. "There was plenty of poverty in the south. In many places there still is."

"All the money goes to the north. There's nothing left for here," says Rosanna, her voice getting a bit sharper. "And the northerners look down on the south. They think the people here are backward."

"It's a little like that in America," I say. "But you have some beautiful towns here. Martina Franca—we loved it. And Lecce—"

"We even found a tennis club there," John interjects. "It was in this walled garden full of statues. Beautiful. I could live in that city. There was this young woman taking a tennis lesson—"

"Right," I interrupt. "You're always watching the pretty women. We walked all around the city. So many beautiful buildings with balconies and flowers. I noticed there were a lot of clocks. On buildings, on towers, on stores. But the funny thing was—the only one with the correct time was the huge sundial in the piazza near the amphitheater!" A laugh from the group. "We couldn't locate a Garibaldi statue though."

John says, "I asked around, and finally someone told us to go to Villa Comunale, the public gardens. That's where we finally found him."

"Him and about thirty others. Not a big monument, just a bust. I kind of expected something more grand in a big city like Lecce."

Roseanna shrugs. "He's not so revered here. A lot of people wish he'd never come back to Italy. Never fought for unification."

This is new.

"Why?" I ask.

"Things were much better here before the Risorgimento. People had money, were prosperous."

"Naples was the wealthiest city in Italy before unification," says Agata. "The center of the Kingdom of the Two Sicilies."

I'm remembering the Naples we saw a couple years ago. The one I didn't care for much. At the street level all the beautiful buildings were carved up with ugly store facades and litter scattered the sidewalks. Maybe it was just where we were, but it didn't feel at all wealthy. It felt dangerous. Especially when the police locked the doors of the museum while we were there because of a riot outside.

"It's still my favorite city," Agata adds. "I loved my time there at university."

Roseanna returns to her history story. "Garibaldi threw the Neapolitans out of Sicily. Then he crossed over from Messina into Calabria and on into Naples. The people there gave him a hero's welcome. But at the end of the war, he handed the south over to the northern king. So, like so many times before, we traded one king for another. And the north stole the wealth. They emptied the treasuries and took everything but the land. And so the people were left with only farming. All the big industry is in the north now. They don't want to invest down here. They think we're beneath them. And so many of our young people have no future unless they leave. Unification did nothing to help *us*. So why celebrate Garibaldi?

"You sound a lot like some of the southerners in America," John says. "They still want to fight the Civil War."

Rosanna sighs. "We were better off before Garibaldi."

So what's the point of all those statues? Are they monuments to the man or the country? Does a revolution need a symbolic face to be understood? Has Garibaldi, like Uncle Sam, become more brand than man? What would America be without Washington, Jefferson, Madison, Adams? Three of them were slave owners but, because of the values they wrote into our founding documents, we overlook it. We cemented their words and now argue about their true intentions. And yet, every child knows Washington as the Father of our Country. That cherry tree story, and Abe Lincoln's woodchopping are threads in the fabric of our oral history. We want these men to be idealists, honest, fair and good. The rest gets pushed under the rug.

"Don't you think societies need heroes?" I ask.

"If not Garibaldi, who?" says John. "Certainly not Mussolini," and everyone laughs. "You'd have to go back to the Romans for a name the world would recognize."

"Augustus," Andrea says. We all agree.

"Italy is defined more by its art than its history," says Francesco.

"Michelangelo," I say.

"Dante," says Andrea.

"Verdi," says Roseanna.

"Galileo," John says.

"You celebrate your artists, your composers and great thinkers," I say. "It's rare to find stone tributes to those kinds of people in America. But we all need heroes—or at least their myths."

Dusk is settling when we slowly return to our little house in Conversano, sad to be leaving the town we've come to like so much. Our footsteps are the only sound on the empty street. The few street lamps illuminate their stone surroundings with a silvery shimmer. Shutters closed tight against the night, no light escapes the windows above. The place feels sturdy and peaceful—unchanged for centuries.

As we pass the closed doorway where the little man would sit in his wheelchair, we notice a paper tacked to it. There's a photo of him and a long text.

John pulls out his reading glasses and squints in the darkness. "He died," he says sadly.

"Oh, *no!*"

"Italians always put these posters up when someone passes. We've seen them before. Their form of obituary."

"Can you read what it says about him?"

"Born in Conversano…family members…worked as a mason, blah, blah. Wait, there's something about the war. Looks like he fought as a Partigiano."

"Really? He probably knew Giuseppe Battista and the other old soldiers. What a shame we didn't stop to speak with him." I pause, regretful, recalling the times we passed and waved. "I'm sure he would have enjoyed it. He probably had some good stories."

John's nodding. "I'll bet he did. Never know what's right under your nose. He might have told us what it was like hiding out in the hills, fighting guerilla-style." We turn toward our own front door where John fumbles with the big key.

Another missed opportunity. We didn't take the time. Didn't stop to acknowledge the history right in front of us. I don't remember the "good" wars—the ones our whole country got behind, willingly sacrificed, believed in. I don't think we'll see them again. It's easy to rush past older folks. After all, we don't want to admit we're coming closer to their age. *I'm still young enough. I work out—most days. There's time to do more. Or is that Baby Boomer optimism?* But I can't help thinking about the impression my footsteps will leave. *Will anyone remember?*

Who *do* people remember? Family, friends, teachers, mentors—those who shaped our lives for good or other. Famous people: Shakespeare, Gandhi, Helen Keller, and OJ Simpson. *What makes a person famous?* Someone writes about them in books, or blogs, or scripts. It helps if the writer is famous too. Like Dumas. He used his own fame to enhance Garibaldi's. Ordinary soldiers, like Giuseppe Battista and his elderly comrades, have been relegated to the background, their causes forgotten. Like them, most heroic people go unremembered—because there's no one to write about them. We aren't famous. But maybe my few words here give Giuseppe Battista and the little man—whose name I don't even recall— a bit of remembrance for their heroism.

CONQUERING NAPLES

Naples. No pen can describe the scene; the whole population thronged the station. Bands, banners, bandieri, National Guards, carriages, ladies of rank and station attired in their white dresses, trimmed with Garibaldian colors, pink and white—thousands of male and female lazzaroni—every human being in the city almost formed the procession to the Palazzo Angri, and there he is installed, and shows himself at the windows. The shouts of "Viva Garibaldi," "Viva Italia Una!" are deafening, and thousands crowd the staircases and spacious saloons of this beautiful palace.

EDWIN JAMES, *NEW YORK TIMES*, SEPTEMBER 8, 1860

NAPLES, ITALY

After subduing Sicily, Garibaldi and his Red Shirts immediately set their sights on Naples, the crown jewel of the Bourbon Kingdom. On August 18, 1860, with the help of British Navy protection they crossed to the mainland. In typical Garibaldi fashion, the action moved fast. Calabria fell on the twenty-first. After a brief fight, the Neapolitan force facing the Straits of Messina surrendered. On August 30, ten-thousand Royalist troops under General Ghio surrendered without firing a shot. Near Padula, General Caldarelli surrendered with three-thousand troops. On the same day the Bourbon King, Francis II, fearing a populist revolt, decided not to try to defend Naples. The garrison

of Salerno was ordered to retreat; on September 6, King Francis II and Queen
Maria Sophia left Naples for the fortress of Gaeta. The Royal army followed,
heading towards Capua.

The next day, September 7, Garibaldi along with a handful of his field
officers, all of them wearing red shirts boarded a train in Salerno headed for
Naples. At 1:30 p.m., the party arrived at the main Naples station—now called
Garibaldi Station located in Piazza Garibaldi— where he was welcomed by the
mayor, twelve thousand armed members of the National Guard, and a crowd of
admirers, all cheering *Viva Garibaldi*.

Like Garibaldi, I arrive in Naples by train from Salerno. But, I'm not feeling much like a conquering hero. First of all, I'm alone. This morning, while I
was boarding for Naples, Nancy caught the train to Rome for a meeting with
Georgina, a Roman friend considering relocation to the States. I'm not entirely
sure how Nancy feels about traveling alone, but for me there's a decided uneasiness.
Second, due to a nasty flare-up of plantar fasciitis in my right foot, I'm forced to
wear a brace and use a cane. Third, the conductor tried to fine me for not having
my ticket stamped. When I explained I had inserted the ticket into the machine
in Salerno, and heard it stamp, he became more insistent saying, in effect, that it's
not sufficient to hear the stamp, you need to check to see if the stamping machine
actually produced a stamp. At which point, I came close to stamping his head with
my cane. Fortunately, for the officious jerk in my face, two young Russian women
showed him their tickets had only the slightest indication of a stamp.

You would think that would have settled the matter. But, it wasn't until others on the train, real Neapolitan commuters not Russian domestics, confirmed
the "stupid" machine in Salerno was seriously defective, did the conductor
finally relent on giving me a fine. That's when the debate really heated up. This is
Italy where not everything works as it's supposed to, but where everything works
for the best. In this case, to the huddled masses on this particular train car, the
malfunctioning machine was one more example, indeed proof, the government's
attempt at cutting costs by automating certain routine jobs was sure to backfire.
In the half hour it took us to reach Naples, there was general agreement that
what the Italian train system needed most was not faster trains and automated

ticketing but better employees, like our handsome conductor in his pressed blue shirt, capable of handling delicate situations for those too feeble—like the old man with the cane— to navigate a system replete with soulless robots.

Now, as I exit the train, I do so with the distinct feeling that the morning's three distinguishing elements—no Nancy, my cane, and the conductor incident—have structured themselves into a bright neon sign on my back that says *Hey everyone, I'm an old tourist, frail and alone; please knock me down and take my wallet.*

Don't get me wrong, I love Naples. Wonderful food. Great museums. Beautiful city. Way too much graffiti, but beautiful. Still, the Naples train station is notorious for pick-pockets and thugs. Were it not for the fact that today was the only day I could work out a meeting with Arigo, I would have gone with Nancy to Rome.

Ah, there he is waving to me: Arigo.

"John, *Eccola.* Here. *Eccola.*"

"Arigo, *come stai, amico?* How are you?"

Arigo. Arigo Ginsberg. He comes from a Jewish family who have lived in Rome for over four hundred years. The best way I can describe him is Brad Pitt. Not that he looks anything like the hunky movie star. No, Arigo is darker, shorter, and less athletic looking. But, like Brad, when it comes to women, Arigo has that certain something.

Look at him. Jacket draped cape-like over his shoulders. Starched, white shirt. Red tie. Pointy black shoes, perfectly shined. Wavy black hair, razor-cut to an intentional muss. Clean shaven. Rimless glasses. Striking blue eyes. Who is this person? Is he a famous model here to shoot a fragrance ad for Armani?

No, he's a PhD economist here to meet an old friend—so old he needs to walk with a cane.

Hugging me, he says, "John, you look great. What's with the cane?"

I return his hug. "It's just a tennis injury. No big deal."

"John, if you can't walk far, we could have a bite there in the McDonald's."

"Oh, no you don't. This town has the best food in the world. I know we don't have much time, but I'm not settling for a Big Mac."

"Okay, John. Okay. I know a place close by."

A short walk from the train station, we enter pizzeria Da Pellone. Who can resist a pizza in the town that invented it? I've not been before, but if Arigo says it's good, I know it has to be. The decor is basic, no-frills; the clientele appears to be mostly locals. Arigo is the only one in the place wearing a suit and tie; and, I'm the only one with a cane. Neither of us looks out of place. But, like the old days, it's Arigo who gets the stares. Women. They sense his presence, then lock on.

We each order a Margherita pizza and a Peroni beer. While we wait for our food, we sip our beers and catch up on old times. We met over thirty years ago when I was V.P. of marketing for Chase Bank's economic consulting arm and Arigo was a senior economist. During the twenty-plus years we haven't seen each other, Arigo has managed to build a stellar career as a professional economist, including positions at the IMF, the London School of Economics, and for the last eight years a VP at the World Bank. I learn he's divorced for the third time, his three children are grown; his oldest girl is a concert pianist living in New York; his son is an architect in Milan; and, his youngest an aspiring actress.

I'm having fun reminiscing about the old days. There was that time when Arigo was chairing a conference in Rome and our bank's foreign exchange forecasting expert missed his plane. Arigo, asked me to pinch-hit, which I did only to find myself speaking after future Nobel Prize winner, Eugene Fama. Arigo and I could laugh at it now, but at the time Fama with loads of facts, stats and original research on his side, told the audience foreign exchange forecasting was a fool's game. When it was my turn to speak, I did a verbal tap dance, showed a few slides, and said something amounting to *and so's your old man*. Immediately after the conference, one of our Italian clients told Arigo to please keep the fat fees they'd already paid for our Forex Services but tell the boss—that would be me—to please do not send them any more forecasts. Using them for the past two years had already cost his firm way too much money. Ouch.

Our pizzas arrive. Thick, airy crusts. Fresh ingredients. Perfectly cooked. I'm in heaven.

Arigo moves the conversation to our shared interest. "We both know the Italian economy is in deep trouble. It needs radical change; corruption, alone, costs the country a massive sixty billion euros—four percent of GDP—each year.

"*Si, si,*" I say setting my slice down. "Like the time in Torino. When we were visiting Fiat. Those strikers rocked our car so violently, I thought we were going to die. It took all the cash we had to make them stop. What did it cost? A couple hundred bucks?"

"That was a transfer payment," Arigo says with a laugh.

"Hey, you saved our asses. So, tell me how you plan to save Italy."

Arigo takes a sip of his beer, puts the glass down precisely on the same watery ring where it came from, and looks at me intently. "First, let's take Naples. One of the worst cases. Last year, the city's unemployment rate was twenty-two-point-six percent. Youth unemployment is over fifty percent. The social safety nets, and there are many, have drained the city coffers. Naples has more debt than most countries. The city can't pay its bills. Look around. Garbage is everywhere. Meanwhile, do you want to guess how much the Social Services administrator for this district earns a year?"

"Why should I guess, when I know you're going to tell me."

"Close to a million dollars per year. Even the head of the sanitation department earns two hundred fifty thousand dollars plus all he can get under the table from the Camorra (Naples' Mafia.) And, you should see the pensions. Government retirees make more after they retire than when they're supposedly working."

I think to myself, Garibaldi is turning in his grave. When he was retiring to Caprera, King Emanuel II offered him a fat pension. Garibaldi turned it down. Instead, he asked that the money be given to the widows and orphans of his troops lost in battle.

"So, Signore Dottore Ginsberg, what's your solution?"

"Luigi de Magistris, the new mayor, he's my solution. You know, he's a former prosecutor who has a track record of fighting corruption. He's sincere about eliminating waste and corruption."

"Are you telling me, he wants to try Basic Income?" I ask.

"Bravo, John. You know where I'm heading. Basic Income is the answer. I'll tell you how it'll work here, but first a few more facts."

The interruption comes in the form of a young, hot-model-like woman, wearing a tennis dress with green-and-blue Mondrian pattern and matching blue-green tennis shoes. She's kissing Arigo. Hard. On the lips.

"*Ciao, Bella,*" he says. "Tennis in the middle of the day, Lucia? How wonderful for you. How can I get a job like yours? I thought the Mayor could not function without you. Yet, you are playing tennis."

"I'll have you know Arigo, I was playing today for a benefit of Kuminda, the feed the world organization. It's all part of the job."

"Sure, sure, my dear. I know how hard you work. Take a minute or two, join us. Meet my old friend, John Petralia, visiting from the States."

"Hello, Lucia. Very pleased to meet you. Please, sit down."

"No. No. Thank you. I don't want to interrupt. Anyway, I have to return to the office. Arigo is right, the mayor is useless without me. I must go. We'll see you later this week, Arigo. The mayor likes your plan. I think we can make it happen. *Ciao, ciao.*"

This time she kisses Arigo on the top of his head, waves good-bye to me, and slips away.

"Arigo, I see nothing has changed with you. Women are still chasing you. If they're all like Lucia, I'd say you are doing just fine, old buddy."

"Oh, she's merely a business associate. A top aide to the Mayor, and very smart. I think she has a boyfriend. Anyway, I'm getting too old for that stuff."

"Bullshit!"

He laughs. "Well, sometimes, for business, one has to do what one has to do. Anyway, what were you asking me?"

"I can't remember. All I can think about is Lucia. Wow. Wow. Wow. Beautiful. I want to know more about how she fits in with the politics here and your economic plans, but first tell me, how's her tennis game?"

"Ha. As a matter of fact, she's really good. Last year, she was Flavia's partner in the Rome Pro-Am. I played with Vinci."

Did I hear that right? "Flavia Pennetta? Roberta Vinci? You know them?"

"John, John, this is *Arigo*. I know people."

"Nothing you say ever surprises me. Not only do you know the tennis stars, but, more important, you know Lucia who can help you get the mayor's support. Impressive."

"Hey, I don't mind telling you. She's been a big help to me."

"I can believe that. She seems—how to say it—competent. But, enough about your conquests. Tell me about Basic Income? Isn't it just another entitlement added to a system that's already insolvent?"

"No, John. Actually, the way we plan it, Basic Income would eliminate many different services such as unemployment benefits, food assistance, child care services, etc. As long as the recipient is seeking a job, the stipend will continue. If there's no attempt to find work, the stipend stops after one year. But here's my innovation: The stipend continues even after employment. So, there's always an incentive to find a job or start a business. Equally important, by eliminating other programs there's less need for bureaucrats. Fewer bureaucrats means fewer regulations, less graft. All good for the economy."

"So, it's like a negative income tax. If you don't have enough to live on, instead of paying taxes, you're given a monthly income."

"Right. The program is currently being tried in Finland. Last year, under my urging, we tried it in Livorno. So far so good. Now, I want to get it going in Naples."

"I understand. So, are you telling me the mayor is ready to change a bloated welfare system that has been around since the end of World War II?"

"I believe so."

Arigo's confidence reminds me of the line from *Il Gattopardo*, *The Leopard*. After Garibaldi handed Naples over to King Victor, the Leopard supported the new regime by saying: *If we want things to remain as they are, everything will have to change.* Arigo and I both know whatever changes are instituted, little will change for the Mayor, Lucia and the the ruling elites. They will still have their afternoon tennis parties and their Maseratis.

"And you, Arigo? What about you?"

He laughs. "Who knows? If Basic Income works in Naples, you Americans just might want to try it in the States. I'd love to get back to Washington. It's still one of my favorite cities. I miss all those parties."

"Ha! Let's take it a step at a time, *amico*. Before you start draining our swamp, let's first see how you make out in Naples."

"Oh, I'll get it done, John. It won't happen overnight, but I'm confident."

I think to myself. If Garibaldi could take Naples without firing a single shot, why can't Arigo?

THE HERO'S HOME

Could slavery not be abolished? If this war is not being fought to emancipate slaves, it would appear to be like any civil war in which the world at large would have little interest or sympathy.

GIUSEPPE GARIBALDI, SEPTEMBER, 1861

CAPRERA, ITALY

The road from Maddelena to Caprera traverses a low jetty across the Tyrrhenian Sea. In Garibaldi's time the Sardinian island was accessible only by boat and so he built a long open one to ferry supplies to the home he constructed here. That home is the goal of our exploration today. He lived all over the world but this is the place Garibaldi chose for his home. The island is wild and hard, like the man. When he came here in 1855 it probably looked much as today, covered in low scrub vegetation and trees whipped by the violent winds that also sculpt the granite rocks. Isolated and rocky, it's not a place most men would choose. But Garibaldi was a warrior, and Mother Nature must have seemed a worthy adversary.

"There's nothing here but Garibaldi's home and a museum," Giuliano says from the driver's seat. He and John have been chatting away in Italian up front while Teresa and I mangle each other's language in the back. "It's all a national park now. But once there was a Club Med." *A Club Med?* I imagine suntanned Europeans splashing around Garibaldi's landing site, drinks in hand, and partying into the night. The idea seems to disrespect the man. I'm glad it closed.

"Hey, look at that," I say, pointing to a warning sign along the road: *Vietato dar da mangiare ai cinghiali.* No feeding the wild boar. In big letters just above it another sign reads *CINGHIALI.* But the red-outlined, triangular graphic topping the word has a silhouette of—a leaping deer.

"Now that's crazy," I say, pointing again so Teresa sees it too. "Why do you think they don't have a boar up there? It's not like this is the only place you can find them. There are plenty of *cinghiali* all over Italy."

Giuliano tosses his comment over his shoulder. "There's probably a problem printing a sign with the correct image. Yes, there are plenty of wild boars in Italy, but it's unusual to see them on the roads."

"It's Italy," John adds. "Accuracy isn't that important." He gets a laugh.

"Yes, but Italians can read the words," I say. "The pictures are what helps *tourists* know what to do. I wonder how many non-Italian visitors are watching out for deer—and feeding the *cinghiali?*" *Doesn't anyone care about sending the entirely wrong message?*

"Do you think non-Italians come here?" John asks. "Or even many Italians for that matter. Have you been here before, Giuliano?"

Our friend shrugs. "Teresa and I have been coming here since 1980, sometimes sailing or in a dingy from Palau, but it was mostly for the beach," he says. "There's a lovely one at the opposite end of the island where we like to swim. We went to Garibaldi's home once or twice, but it's been a long time. It wasn't much as I recall." As our unofficial guides in Italy, Teresa and her husband have shown us dozens of places other people miss. It would be great if we could reciprocate. But the truth is, they've seen more of America than we have.

Our road winds upward through the vegetation until we can see the water in the distance. Giuliano pulls the car onto the berm and the four of us get out for a good look. When the door opens, the sweet fragrance of herbs and flowers is carried on the constant breeze. Spindly pines are scattered among the low brush, their trunks exposed with only a broccolini-like ruffle of green at the top. Giuliano has his long lens trained on the view back toward the causeway and Maddelena. I'm satisfied after three or four photos, but Giuliano remains for five minutes, turning left and right to capture every scene.

We arrive at the parking area for the Garibaldi home and leave the car. I notice a red-painted souvenir stand as we near the path to the house. Of course I want a good remembrance of Garibaldi's home, so I head straight for it. Not much bigger than a flea market table it offers coral necklaces, a decorative wooden anchor, terra cotta olive oil servers, a seashell-coated photo frame, baseball caps in a variety of colors stamped with "Caprera." The Sardinian emblem, showing the four blindfolded Moors, is emblazoned on key chains, pot holders, tiny ceramic bells, coasters, plates, mugs and scarfs. Hung in the center of the rear wall is an ornamental life preserver, with a map of Sardinia mounted inside, and "Welcome Aboard"—in English—written around the edge. Next to it is a circular plaque featuring Tom and Jerry, the Hanna-Barbera cartoon cat and mouse. *Huh?*

In the center of the table is a modest poster for two euros. It features several pictures and paintings of Garibaldi and one of a statue on a hilltop. In its center is printed *Giuseppe Garibaldi, Caprera, la mia isola,* my island. *That's it? Where's the red shirt? The pillbox hat? Or even a copy of one of his hundreds of statues? How about a t-shirt for the Hero of Two Worlds* John asks the Pakistani vendor where we might find something else about Garibaldi and gets an indifferent shrug.

"Amazing," I say to him. "Let's try the building over there where the restrooms are. Looks like there's a shop next to them." We trot over and pull the door open. Not much of a shop. Just a small room with a freezer for ice cream bars, cold drinks, and snacks. No souvenirs in sight. "Maybe there's more at the house," I say to John as we start down the path toward it.

Flowering shrubs have been planted along the walkway among the granite boulders. An enormous old tree grows laterally, flattened by winds in its youth. A sign explains Garibaldi put up a windmill, but had to remove it because the gales were too strong. A battle he lost to Mother Nature.

John seems particularly pokey today, taking my hand to slow my pace on the descent toward the house. He looks preoccupied. We've been traveling a long time and it may be wearing on him. "Do you think this is the same path

Sanford took when he came to visit?" I ask. My husband has read so much about Garibaldi. I'm hoping the question will pull him back into the experience. It'll also give him a chance to share some American history with Giuliano.

"Probably. In 1861 Sanford would have come over by boat and walked to the house. He was on a mission from Lincoln."

"From Lincoln?" says Giuliano.

"*Si.* In 1861 Ambassador Sanford was already in Europe charged with keeping France, England and Spain from entering the war as 'peacekeepers'—or recognizing the Confederacy. Either would assure independence for the secessionist states. Sanford came here in September of that year, not long after Bull Run. The Union thought that battle would end the war. Instead Stonewall Jackson earned his nickname and sent the Union soldiers running back to Washington DC Lincoln was in trouble.

"In Italy, the country's Unification was nearly completed and Garibaldi had retired back to Caprera. At the time he was probably the most famous man in the world—hailed as the Unifier of Italy and before that Defender of Montevideo. There were already statues of him in South America in 1861. The Italians were busy renaming streets and melting bronze for their newly inaugurated piazzas. Alexander Dumas was lauding him in stories, and in the New York Tribune, Horace Greely was crying 'Bully for Garibaldi' urging the president to bring him to head the Union army."

"So what happened?" our friend asks.

"Lincoln gave Garibaldi an offer he had to refuse.

"But why?"

"It's a great question. You see, Garibaldi believed in equality and freedom. Many of his fighters in South America were slaves he freed. He told Sanford he'd be pleased to lead the Union army, but he had just one question. Was the war about freeing the slaves?"

Giuliano has a quizzical look. "Well wasn't it? Lincoln did free them."

"Not then. The Union had four slave states—Missouri, Kentucky, Delaware and Maryland. In his first election, Lincoln even ran on a platform that said he had no legal authority to free the slaves. In 1861, if he'd done so, the president would have lost those states—and that would have been the end of the Union. So Sanford went back home—without Garibaldi. Nonetheless, Garibaldi would continue to figure prominently in world events, including the Civil War."

We've come to the compound's entrance where there's merely a ticket booth, no souvenir shop. With several other people we wait at the gate until a young woman guide joins us. Dressed in a dark skirt and white blouse, she wears neither jewelry nor a smile. Speaking only in Italian she refers to Garibaldi as The Hero.

"Do you speak English also?" I ask.

"*Italiano*," she says dismissively. *This is going to be a challenge.*

She begins our tour in the courtyard where the arms of massive trees are twisted like wind-blown tresses. Several small white buildings ring the perimeter. *I wonder what they are.* There's no time to look around. Our guide is already into the old barn. "No photos," she instructs us sternly. Amid the collection of farming and fishing tools is a steam-powered vehicle with big metal wheels Garibaldi used to haul supplies from his landing site up the hillside to his home. Two saddles he brought from South America are here, and on the wall a plaque serves as headstone over where his beloved horse, Marsala, is buried. Most unusual though is a six-foot copper bathtub. The guide says he liked bathing out here. *Maybe all the years of camping on battlegrounds made him uncomfortable inside the house?* There's not much time to look around as our guide is marching out and off to the modest stone home Garibaldi called the "White House."

In the entrance hallway she breezes through a recitation about the rifles and photos, points to the red upholstered wheelchair and turns into the next room. As we're moving after her I notice a strange contraption. John and I scrutinize and decide it's a folding camp chair like the English would take on safari. He must have used it on the march.

The next room is a bedroom first used by the Hero's daughter and, after her marriage, became his own bedroom. Covering the ornate iron bed is a red spread. Some kind of folding bench, also upholstered in red, is jammed up against the footboard. The guide speaks really fast and I'm struggling to catch anything of what she's saying. On the wall is a collection of photos. I enjoy putting faces onto historic names and I'd like to peer at some of them, but there isn't time. Once her memorized speech is finished she turns on her heel and heads for the next room. *Wait. Wait. Let us look around.* As we're leaving, John tells me she mentioned a braid of hair from Garibaldi's first wife Anita is mounted on the wall. Wish I could have seen it.

Now we're in Manilo's bedroom. He was Garibaldi's youngest son, born when the Hero was sixty-six. *Sixty-six. That means Manilo was only 15 when his father died.* A slight child, his father doted on him sharing stories of his adventures on the sea. Garibaldi could do just about anything he set his mind to: *I wonder if he made the model ships here for his son to play with.* Manilo's slender military uniform hangs in a glass case and another red blanket covers his iron bed. Like many young people of the time, he died of tuberculosis at twenty-seven. His young sister Rosa had died of whooping cough at the age of two, leaving only Clelia, the eldest of Garibaldi's third union.

Her bedroom is next. It was Clelia who worked to preserve the home for the memory of her father. More fortunate than her youngest brother, she lived ninety-two years, until 1959. Once again, the bedspread is red and photos of Clelia with her father hang on the wall. I see framed certificates on the wall too. I'll ask about them. No, I won't. Rushing on, the guide spurs us to the kitchen, again without pausing for questions.

Since I love to cook, I'm always interested in old kitchens and I wonder what their cooking life was like. Unlike the other rooms, this one's not crowded with unrelated articles. For its time and remote locale, it appears well-equipped with a water pump, a red-tiled stove and backsplash, and a fireplace with a spit roaster. White tile covers the sink wall and copper pots hang on a rack. The big window and the white paint make it cheery and I can imagine myself preparing a meal here. But I won't be able to daydream about it because after a few rapid sentences our guide has moved on.

The dining room has been turned into a sort of museum with the dining table, breakfront and red upholstered love seat pushed back into one corner. *Did HE love red fabric that much?* Portraits of Garibaldi's children and his third wife, Francesca Armorsino, hang on one wall. Display cabinets hold his crutches, walking sticks and an umbrella. The long wall displays his clothing: the signature red shirt, a kind of poncho in tan, and what reminds me of a priest's cape, red-lined white with gold trim. Next to it is a series of drawings showing his wounded foot—sustained in the battle of Aspromonte—and in front of them, his red-upholstered wheelchair. In the center of the room is a cabinet with other personal items. I notice a bullet, a pair of binoculars, glasses, a letter with signature, a boot and an ankle brace among the items. The guide finishes spewing rapid-fire Italian then whirls for the doorway.

"Mi scusi," I call to her and point to the eyeglasses. *"Questi sono i suoi occhiali?"* These were his? She stops and gives me an irritated look.

"Si."

I notice a few waxy candles in the case and before she can retreat I try again. "These candles," I grope in Italian, "did he make them? We visited Muecci's home on Staten Island in America where Garibaldi lived and worked in Muecci's candle factory."

She's glaring. *"Li ha fatti."* He made them.

How long can I keep this up? My mind is whirling to organize Italian grammar. *"E questa lettera è stata scritta da Lui?"* He wrote the letter?

"Si. L'ha scritto lui. Si può vedere la sua firma." Yes, he wrote it. You can see his signature.

I don't dare look down yet. She's turning to leave so I point to the brace. I'm determined to make her spend a few moments here. To answer a few questions. To acknowledge the patrons. *"E questo è per il suo piede ferito?"* It's for his wounded foot?

"Si," she says with a harrumph, then rattles off some rapid Italian I can't understand. Something about the 1862 battle in Aspromonte where he got shot. Then she scurries into the next room. At least I pulled a few unscripted words out of her. I've won a skirmish if not the war.

The study is next. Over the fireplace is a portrait of Rosita, his daughter by Anita who was born in Uruguay and only lived four years. This must have doubled as a music room too because an organ, a phonograph and a piano are here along with a writing desk and a beautiful chest of drawers. I remember reading he had a player piano shipped here, hauled it up the hillside, and put it together himself. There's a story about Clelia too. Although the Caprera home was isolated, people often came to visit the Hero. As a young girl, shy Clelia would hang back whenever he had guests. One evening Garibaldi saw her and realized she was feeling left out. Taking her hands, her father danced her around the house until their laughter lifted her spirits. It was a lively folk dance, and everyone was amazed at what an accomplished dancer he was.

All the rooms of the house are painted white. Dark wood trim and window frames give the house a clean, modern look. The furniture is quite fine for an island home. He obviously cared about the quality of his family's environment and brought the best things and most modern technologies here. It's not a grand home, but the rooms are bigger than I would have guessed. It's hard to tell, though, with all the artifacts crammed in. When Garibaldi lived here it must have been a comfortable house. A house I think I could live in even now.

We've come to the final room, the one where Garibaldi died. It was added to the house in his later years to accommodate family and friends who came to visit. With windows on three sides and an arched exit doorway, it's a cheerful room. In his final days the Hero asked to be moved here. His bed was placed facing a large window with a view to Corsica and his birthplace of Nice. Shortly after he died the bed was surrounded by a bronze balustrade to protect it from enthusiastic visitors and pilgrims. His son Menotti stopped the clock on the wall at the exact time of death, 6:20 p.m. Next to it another shows the date, June 2, 1882. His last will is mounted here. In it he asked to be cremated. Two red-upholstered sofas sit against the walls for the visitors in his final days. His wheelchair with the writing arm stands next to the bed, and one of his most famous portraits hangs on a wall. On the nightstand is a handkerchief, embroidered with the letter A. When the guide says it stands for Anita, the Hero's first wife, John whispers to me, "No way. She wouldn't have had something so frilly." This is a beautiful room, the only one preserved as it was. It's peaceful. I linger long after our guide has hurried from the building, staring out the window as Garibaldi no doubt had done.

When I finally step outside and down the short walkway to the garden gate everyone has moved on. Opposite, perched on a rise, sits a small round building with a narrow door and conical, cooper roof. It's cute, and reminds me of a *trullo. Could it be an outhouse?* There wasn't any plumbing facility inside. And in 1882 they probably didn't have any. I hope it isn't the outhouse, for not fifteen feet away is a half-statue of the Hero. His characteristic scarf is knotted around his neck and his hands gather his cloak tight against the wind. He's looking off to his left, in the direction of Nice.

I finally catch up with the group at the little cemetery. Here, in direct contradiction to his personal wishes, Giuseppe Garibaldi, Hero of Two Worlds, is buried in a granite tomb. He's surrounded by family in traditional above-ground vaults. His, though, is massive and appears like a natural boulder, weathered like the terrain. On the top, simply GARIBALDI.

At the end of the path our only option is to exit the grounds through another gate. There's no way to get back to the lovely courtyard and explore the other buildings. Or to linger in the place the Hero loved. Just a one-way trip. *Finito e arrivederci.* Finished and goodbye.

"So where were all his books, John? Didn't you tell me he read a lot?"

"He did. All kinds of things. I think he had over three thousand books. Funny none of them are in the house anywhere."

"No room for that many in the house. Maybe they moved them. But it would have been nice to leave a bookcase full, or even to mention his extensive library."

Many things perplex me about this place. Clelia lived in the house until her death in 1959 and was dedicated to preserving her father's home. She obviously kept many of his personal belongings so they could be displayed here. I can't help thinking he wouldn't be pleased with all the emphasis on his infirmities: the wheelchairs, braces, crutches and such. From paintings and drawings, I know he worked this property, but except for a few implements in the barn, there's no sense of the Hero as tamer of this land. I can imagine him, strong and driven, harnessing the force of his muscles and will to fell the trees, dig the rocky soil, plant the olive and fig trees, and haul the rocks and manure for his crops. I see him rowing his boat from Maddelena, loading supplies onto a wagon and firing up his locomotor to haul them up the hillside with maybe a new musical instrument aboard. And I envision him, with family gathered around a piano, singing. But nothing in this home's presentation *helped* me imagine that.

I keep thinking of our visits to the homes of our Founding Fathers. In Mount Vernon, Monticello or the Hermitage there's a sense of the living man who occupied them. Rooms are set as they were in the original time with books and pipe stands, lamps and footstools in place. The table is set and the inkwell and open ledger are on the desk. If there's an unusual artifact in place, it's because Washington or Jefferson put it there. I imagine this house was a modest but comfortable home when Garibaldi lived here. I wish I could walk through it and feel him inside. Instead, the jumble of artifacts crowds out his humanity.

The most glaring difference, though, is the way our tour was conducted. The volunteers who guide thousands through the homes of Washington, Jefferson and Jackson seem to love what they do and are eager to share their knowledge. They may be on a time schedule, but you never feel herded, and if you ask about something you notice in a room, they're happy to tell you about it. You're encouraged to walk about the outbuildings to talk with other docents or to get a feel for the labor that took place there at working exhibits. There's pride and reverence in their manner that's missing here. It makes me sad. Instead of getting an appreciation for the way Garibaldi lived on Caprera, I feel I've been peeking into an attic where his things are stashed.

While Giuliano poses Teresa in front of a big rock, John and I muse about the experience as we walk back to the car. "We've been looking for Garibaldi, but he certainly wasn't *here*." I say. "Not even in his own home."

"Maybe all that's left of him is a myth."

"We still venerate Lincoln and Washington. Hold them up as heroes, but also real people. That guide was so dismissive. Maybe it was just her, but the larger message of this place is like a Roman ruin, dusty and discarded."

"It's like so much of his life. Victories turning to tragedy."

Rain pelts our car as we leave Caprera and head back to Maddelena then dials back once we reach the outskirts. It's not an ancient town. Most of it was built in the 18th century. Along the waterfront, where the ferry from Palau docks beside fishing boats, runs a wide boulevard punctuated with small parks.

"Who's this?" I ask John when we discover a bronze half-statue topping a rough granite stone. The slender, patrician-looking gentleman is hatless, but wears a loose-fitting shirt over an inner one. Around his shoulders is knotted a large bandana. Only his left hand is visible. The plaque imbedded in the stone beneath him reads in Italian:

The most faithful of Garibaldi
Giovanni Battista Culiolo,
"Greater Light"
National Association of Garibaldini
on the Centennial of the Unity of the Commune of Maddelena
1861-1961

My husband looks puzzled. "He's not someone I'm familiar with. Probably a local guy. He may have been a confidant to Garibaldi as he was plotting his attacks on Sicily and the mainland." *Did he conspire with Garibaldi at the Hero's home? Could he have been one of the thousand?* He must be pretty important to have this statue here. "Can you find him online?" John asks me.

I tap for a few moments, then summarize what's on the screen. "He was a great friend of Garibaldi. Born here in Maddelena. He followed Garibaldi to Uruguay and fought with him in Montevideo. Then he was one of the sixty-three who returned with him to fight in Rome in 1848. Quite the hero himself, he was wounded badly in Rome." I glance again at the statue. "Maybe he lost his right arm? Anyway, when he learned the French had driven Garibaldi out of Rome, Culiolo left the hospital in search of his general. He finally caught up to the Hero in Cesenatico. Anita was quite ill at the time and she died a few days later. It says Culiolo offered great support to his grieving friend, spurring him on "for your children, for Italy."

"Well, I can understand why he's memorialized here." John takes my arm as we move on, his weight shifting onto me with every step of his left foot.

From the waterfront we walk up into the town. Here and there a white structure disrupts the typical red, orange, and shades of yellow ochre of the town's buildings. Several in the oldest part are decorated with iron balconies, window trims and round-top shutters. A rectangular sundial crowns the plain facade of the yellow stucco church. Inside, we're surprised to find beautiful mosaics in each of the niches along the sides, their tiny almost iridescent tiles sparkling.

Teresa wants to get a *caffè* so, exiting the church, we part from our friends to explore on our own. In a small piazza we discover Garibaldi—a life-sized, bronze Garibaldi sitting on a curved marble bench. His left hand clutches his hat across his thigh while his right hand is balanced on his walking stick. The ubiquitous scarf is knotted below his neatly trimmed beard. Though not smiling, his eyes appear warm. The ramrod-straight back makes him look statue-like, as though posed for one of those early portraits where the sitters had to be still for several minutes in front of the open shutter.

"Oh, go sit there, honey," I say. "I'll take your picture with him."

John plunks down, a grin spreading across his face. Snap. Snap. I ask a passerby to take one of the two of us and seat myself on Garibaldi's opposite side. Snap. *So Giuseppe, if I may call you that, what are you thinking? Do you find yourself seated and photographed with folks all the time? How many Americans? Do people even recognize you? Or do they simply think you're an entertaining bronze figure? Fun for a selfie. What do you make of what's happened at your home? Did you really upholster everything in red? How does it feel that they ignored your request to be cremated and keep all those wheelchairs around? Is that how you'll be remembered? A crippled up old man? That's not who you are, is it? Or are you remembered at all?*

I gaze across the small piazza and spy another Garibaldi on an opposite bench. This one is very much alive, smoke trailing from the cigarette dangling in his hand. He's the same size and age as the one between us, but his beard is wilder, streaked with brown and sliver, and his hat's a fishing cap. Slumped down on the bench, legs and athletic shoes extended, his gray pants have a red stripe, perhaps part of a military uniform. Cigarette in hand, he's scowling. *Is he aware of his likeness to the Hero? Does he come here to flaunt a counterpoint?*

We meander down Via Giuseppe Garibaldi, a narrow, pedestrian shopping street, ducking into shops to escape the light rain. Tourism dominates the economy here and we discover all kinds of souvenirs bearing the Sardinian four Moors insignia—the defeated Moors dating back to the 13th century. There are Sardinian flags, t-shirts with English sayings, cork products, jewelry, women's clothing, men's polo shirts, bathing suits and coverups, kites, beach towels and water toys. We find a store with boating supplies and several cafes. But nowhere is there even a mention of Garibaldi.

"I don't get it," I say to John. "This is a huge missed marketing opportunity. People have to come through here to get to Caprera. We didn't find any Garibaldi souvenirs there, so I figured for sure there would be some here in Maddelena."

His eyes widen, his voice exaggerated excitement. "Maybe we could open a shop! We could make up red t-shirts with 'Here we make Italy, or die.' on them. Do up some of those pillbox hats he wore—I'd like one of those. And cool red shirts."

I'm into the game. "We could have embroidered tea towels with 'Caprera' on them like the pretty ones they have in Palau. Or better, with his White House on them. Commemorative plates, coffee mugs, maybe a replica of his boat or toy soldiers. A 'Don't Feed the Cinghali' t-shirt for sure. If we wanted to get really tacky, we could put Anita's picture on some pot holders!" We're both chuckling now.

I point into the window of the next store where printed t-shirts are displayed totem pole style. "Want to get one of those shirts with the *cinghiali* on it, '*Io vivo in Sardegna*,' for someone back home?" I live in Sardinia.

John gestures toward the front of the store. "OK, but you look at the t-shirts on that rack. I think you'd look nice in one of them."

We emerge later with a large shopping bag and catch up with the Vitalis at the bar. "Let's walk down to the harbor," suggests Giuliano. "Maybe we can find someplace for an early dinner."

As we're walking I ask, "Giuliano, why aren't there any Garibaldi souvenirs here. I figured there would be a lot, but we didn't see anything."

"Italians would never buy them," he says without hesitation.

Really? "Why not? It's part of your history."

He shrugs. "People aren't interested in Garibaldi any more."

How strange. I can't imagine Americans not wanting a little piece of Washington from Mount Vernon. Or something to remind them of their visit to Monticello. Both of them have gift shops with books, and replicas of the china, linens and silver the presidents used, and pocket copies of the Constitution. You can get a lovely ornament to decorate your Christmas tree or to hang in a window. Williamsburg makes a fortune selling stuff. *Are we Americans just focused on shopping?* Maybe, but we like having a little piece of the places we visit. We love bobble-heads, magnets and key chains with the Washington monument on them. Italians aren't like that. You don't find a lot of chintzy Chinese trinkets in their stores. Unless there's a soccer game, they don't even fly the Italian flag. But Garibaldi birthed their country. You'd think they'd want a little piece of that.

SEEING RED

Red is such an interesting color to correlate with emotion, because it's on both ends of the spectrum. On one end you have happiness, falling in love, infatuation with someone, passion, all that. On the other end, you've got obsession, jealousy, danger, fear, anger and frustration.

TAYLOR SWIFT

COLUMBIA, SOUTH CAROLINA

The University of South Carolina, home of the Carolina Gamecocks. Everywhere I look, I see red. Red caps. Red shirts. Red banners. Students here love to show their colors.

Garibaldi? South Carolina? What's the connection?

Historian, Dr. Anthony P. Campanella: he's the connection. Born in Sicily and raised in New York, Campanella wanted his collected works and writings on Garibaldi to be used in an academic venue for researchers interested in Garibaldi and the Risorgimento. With its high academic standards and strong focus on international studies, the University met all of Campanella's criteria.

As we enter the Hollings Building where the collection is housed, I am of two minds. First and foremost, I can't wait to get my hands on all the original documents. We're looking to understand Garibaldi, the man—who, what, why and how. But something bothers me about how the university justifies (rationalizes)

187

having the collection located in the heart of the former Confederacy. Here's what the website says about Garibaldi's march from Genoa to Sicily to Naples:

> ...*There can be no doubt that the March, whose progress was eagerly followed in a United States ideologically opposed to European dynastic "tyranny," was viewed in this country as a powerful vindication of the right of the individual to political self-determination. It also encouraged Southern leaders in their move towards secession at precisely the time when accounts of Garibaldi's exploits appeared in the American press. Nor is it coincidental that in 1876 Wade Hampton's followers, in their resistance to the continued presence of Federal troops in South Carolina, appropriated the name of Garibaldi's followers--Red Shirts--for themselves...*

To which, I say, "Huh?"

No, I'm not going to tell the University what their website should say. On the other hand, their attempt to connect disparate histories of Garibaldi and of the Deep South makes me angry. Let's face it, though decidedly on a smaller scale, Garibaldi's march through Southern Italy—unification-by-conquest—is a lot closer to Sherman's March to the Sea than an example of political self-determination. Indeed, to believe the latter, you'd have to also believe Garibaldi would equate slavery with the pursuit of happiness. The fact is Garibaldi was as wild-eyed an abolitionist as one of his heroes, John Brown. In Brazil, Garibaldi's troops raided plantations to free slaves. Ex-slaves served in his armies and navies not only in South America but with the Red Shirts in Italy. Anita, his wife, was mixed-race.

Get real! In 1860, the only way Garibaldi's dark-skinned children would have been seen on this campus would have been as servants. When Lincoln asked him to serve as a general in the Union army, Garibaldi would have accepted if Lincoln would tell him the war was about freeing slaves. While Garibaldi never did get to trade his red shirt for a blue coat, his actions—not always successful—served as stark contrast to both monarchism in Europe and slavery in the Confederacy. Perhaps, most important, Garibaldi showed how liberators could build an army of freed slaves.

To be sure, the University of South Carolina is not the first to piggyback on our hero's broad shoulders. Piedmont's Prime Minister Benso Cavour and King Victor Emmanuele II were past masters at it. In Dante's ranking system, surely they would be found in the Ninth Circle, the one reserved for the most evil of evildoers, the treacherous. Cavour wanted Garibaldi's March to fail so much, he withheld arms and equipment. For Cavour, Garibaldi was no more than a stalking horse. In his mind, there was no way a handful of poorly armed rebels could defeat a well-trained, well-equipped, larger regular army. Besides, Piedmont did not even want Sicily. It certainly did not want the Sicilians. Victor was even more circumspect. When it suited his expansionist purposes, King Victor embraced Garibaldi, called him brother; but after Garibaldi handed over Southern Italy and Sicily, the King marginalized all the Red Shirts, including their leader.

Perhaps the worst offender of the Garibaldi legacy was that other Italian dictator: Mussolini. When Il Duce took what remained of the Papal States, he did so by reminding his countrymen that Garibaldi, too, viewed Rome as the beating heart of Italy.

Of course, there's also the other extreme: those who would have you believe Garibaldi was some sort of cartoon superhero. I put Alexander Dumas and Madame Schwartz in this category. Dumas painted Garibaldi as a sort of fourth musketeer, rushing into battle willy-nilly, no plan, love of the fight, against great odds, always victorious. Reading him is more like reading Cervantes describing Don Quixote. Garibaldi's military exploits may not have been on a par with Caesar, Napoleon or MacArthur, but he was a real person, brave beyond all reasoning, with real feelings. If you prick him, doth he not bleed?

So, here I am at the Hollings' Library. Mixed feelings. But on one thing, there is no debate: the library staff treats Nancy and me like visiting dignitaries, even assigning a student librarian, Robert, to retrieve books and documents for us. The documents are stored in file-sized cardboard bins marked with red letters. Robert allows us one bin at a time. Each bin contains exactly fifty documents individually enclosed in a clear plastic folder open on one end. When we find something particularly noteworthy, Robert allows us to photograph the item with our iPhones but we are not to remove documents from folders. Since we've already read most of the Garibaldi biographies, we're mainly interested in the letters and news articles. Most are in Italian. I can read printed Italian pretty well, but I'm struggling with the handwriting, especially when confronted with the exaggerated swirls and loops characteristic of the period. Even letters written in English are hard to decipher. What is most striking is the esteem Garibaldi engenders from masses of ordinary people. Here's a letter from a British admirer:

Farewell General Garibaldi:

I thank my God that my eyes have gazed upon the noblest man on the earth. For years, your cause has been familiar to all as a household word, and I have prayed with my whole heart for the fulfillment of your most ardent desire. May health and happiness ever be yours and may the savior of Italy live to see her united great glorious and free.

Yours with deepest respect,

L.A. Suregrass, Westminster, April, 1864

There are dozens of letters like this referring to Garibaldi's triumphant trip to London in the spring of 1864. One of my favorites is one written by a former Red Shirt, an Englishman, reminding Garibaldi he was never paid for his services; never mind, he says, it was compensation enough to have served with someone of such greatness. There are letters from several Italian mayors, special awards, proclamations; a French woman desires a lock of his hair; there are scores of invitations to dine; one to go riding; an English woman wants to marry him; another woman needs a job. Pleas for an autograph. Italian women are naming their babies after him. Newspapers around the world laud his accomplishments. Here's an 1862 article from a yellowed French newspaper comparing Garibaldi to Jesus:

Your sacrifice seems a transubstantiation. All of you that was earthly has disappeared with your blood. Your wounds render you divine. Aspromonte recalls the peaks of Calvary, your martyrdom recalls the Passion. Your glory becomes a cult. The people loved you; now they adore you. They glorified you; now they adore you. You were great; now you are a saint. Ecce Homo.

Felix Pyat, *The Paris Commune*.

As I read letter after letter, I think to myself: Thank God for those red pills. Without them, I doubt I could read any of the Garibaldi documents here at the Hollings Library. Customized to my DNA, AREDS are the large red vitamin pills I've been taking for the past year—ever since we started writing this book. No, I don't think the AREDS deserve all the credit for my improved vision, but you better believe I'm not going to stop taking them. And, yes, I still need the occasional injection of Avastin in my right eye, but I've gone from getting stuck every six weeks to every four months. As Leonard Cohen liked to sing: "Hallelujah." Funny thing about the improvement in my vision: Somehow, my vocabulary and my memory have also improved. Nancy says it's because the AREDS allow me to see what I'm saying. I'm not sure about her logic but I get her point. I wish I could tell you the AREDS have miraculously improved my gait and my constipation, but that hasn't happened.

During a break, we chat with, Scott, a young Poly-Sci graduate student working at a table next to us. He is doing his PhD dissertation on Southern Republicans in the twentieth century.

"You're in the right place for that," I say. "I remember Senator Fritz Hollings—seemed quite the proper southern gent. Great drawl. Smart. Gracious. Always wore a white suit. A Southern politician direct from central casting."

"Right you are. That's him. Fritz Hollings is a legend around here. He'll figure prominently in my research. What are the two of you working on?"

"Garibaldi," I say. "Giuseppe Garibaldi."

"I know the name. Remind me who he was."

"The Unifier of Italy. Hero of Two Worlds. One of the greatest men of his time. You Gamecocks would have loved him. He always wore a red shirt."

REMEMBER ME

I wish it to be remembered that I was the last man of my tribe to surrender my rifle.

SITTING BULL

FORT MYERS, FLORIDA

This quest for Garibaldi has steered our lives for nearly two years. I can't help remembering that the day I met him was the day we also met Giuliano and Teresa. John and I were new residents in Bologna and had arranged to meet Giuliano to exchange practice in Italian and English. After a warm greeting, Giuliano in the lead, the four of us set off around the city. Midway down Via Indipendenza he stopped and pointed across the street to the bronze statue on a high pedestal—a bearded, athletic-looking man wearing a loose-fitting shirt and a sort of beret with a scarf knotted around his neck. Not a soldier. I wondered who he was.

"Garibaldi." said Giuliano. "Giuseppe Garibaldi, the Unifier of Italy." That was news to me. I didn't remember studying much Italian history in school. A lot of English history, the French Revolution, the Spanish explorers, something about the Renaissance and a little about the World Wars. *Garibaldi united Italy?*

When we moved to Parma, Piazza Garibaldi became our favorite haunt. His dominant bronze figure in the main square—the meeting point that was otherwise ignored. We met friends and took photos of visitors under his giant

192

statue. Beneath his gaze passed nearly every important city event: foot races, dance exhibitions, health fairs, food festivals, and fireworks. While Parma's Piazza Garibaldi will always be *our* piazza, we soon discovered it was by no means unique.

Like a treasure hunt, when we explored a new city, town, or village, we'd always ask, *"Dove si trova Piazza Garibaldi?"* Where is Piazza Garibaldi? Our compass for getting to know a place, and its people. We might find a monument where folks gathered on the steps or surrounding low wall, panini in hand, to chat during the day. There's a statue of the man in the Piazza Garibaldi of Palermo, Verona, Milan, Pisa, Rome, Padua, Genova, Livorno, La Spezia, Todi, Naples and dozens more cities—even in France's Nice. Smaller towns have a bust or a plaque. Villages too small to afford even that at least have their Via Garibaldi—the ubiquitous avenue named for the Hero of Two Worlds, the soldier who was the Unifier of Italy.

And I began to wonder. How do people remember him?

Nearly seven years later I know the response is mixed. Despite his heroic deeds, his fame, the real man has faded from memory. In Buenos Aires his name is famous—as a cocktail. The victim of declining budgets, his Montevideo home is closed. For many in Italy he exists as a label: Unifier of Italy. And for some, it's an unwelcome moniker. The larger-than-life *man* is forgotten.

In our travels I often look to statues and memorials as indicators of what a society values—at least in the past. Who is immortalized in stone or bronze? What messages do those memorials convey? Surrounding Florence's Uffizi you'll find the greatest artists, writers, thinkers and explorers of Italy. Our presidents on Mount Rushmore. Beside the Washington mall, Martin Luther King. One of my favorite DC memorials, on Constitution Avenue, is the statue of Albert Einstein. Then there's Rocky at the bottom of the Art Museum steps in Philadelphia and Buffalo Bill in Oklahoma City. All heroes in their own way.

So what does "hero" mean today? Is it still the person who is admired or idealized for courage, outstanding achievements, or noble qualities? Perhaps. But in the cacophony of news and Internet and 24/7 coverage, it's hard to pick them out. Heroic figures— Jefferson, Washington, Lincoln, Roosevelt, Martin

Luther King, Giuseppe Garibaldi—ones who inspire soldiers and nations with words and personal bravery, will we ever see their like again? Today's "heroes" are less well known, more relatable; firemen, EMTs, everyman soldiers, 9/11 responders. We anoint the local man who rescues a drowning dog a hero. Certainly a deed worthy of recognition, but does it rise to the level of heroism?

Maybe we don't need real heroes anymore. After all, none of them can live up to the ones we create on screen, in games, or even in novels. It happened even to Garibaldi who grew larger on paper and film. But the man's deeds still stand. The hundreds of statues, thousands of *piazze* and streets still stand. The devotion of his troops was real. The veneration of the people was real. The admiration of nations was real. Not so of Luke Skywalker, Captain America or Daenerys Targaryen. Today's monuments celebrate these fantasy figures in theme parks and 3D worlds for everyone to experience—to *play* the hero for a while.

I always thought of my mother as my hero. But when I'm gone, no one else will remember her. I have no children, so no family will remember me. *Does it matter if our footsteps disappear in the sand? Life is for the living.* Our own journey, our personal quest is what matters most to each of us. This Garibaldi search, shared with the man I love, pulled us into his world—brought us closer to each other.

Many people are heroic in their quiet way, a few on the larger stage. A desire for heroism isn't lost—most of us are looking for some heroes. I know I am. I may not have met the Hero of Two Worlds, but exploring his life has given me new friends across the globe, a discovery of America's past, a new perspective on the present, and adventures of my own.

I'm glad I got to know you, Giuseppe.

ACKNOWLEDGEMENTS

Writing books is hard. Were it not for the weekly comments and critiques provided by members of the Writers' Group at the Fort Myers Regional Library this book would still be a collection of unfinished drafts. Candace Clemens, Mark Lipton, Jim Berger, Geneva Kelly, Patricia Downey, Bill Bower, Stratis Skoufalos, Diane Fowler, Melvia Zeigler, and Ellie Peterson provided unwavering encouragement and insightful advice on style, word choice, and context. We are grateful to the Fort Myers Library especially Courtney Barr for providing our weekly meeting space.

We are indebted to our beta readers John Mastronardo, Sy and Susan Koslowsky, Sybilla Zeldin, Phyllis Ershowsky and Susan Kovacevich for their probity and insight.

Artis Henderson provided careful, intelligent editing. Photographer Patricia Downey and artist Patti Brassard Jefferson created an innovative cover design. Together they make us look like the professional writers we had always hoped to become.

Our travels for this book took us to Argentina where we were befriended by the amazing Rappaport family who helped us find accommodations, fair money exchanges, and the best shopping spots in Buenos Aires. In Uruguay, the staff of the National Historical Museum of Montevideo gave us access to their

Garibaldi collection, helped us understand conditions during the siege of 1843, and broke untold government laws and restrictions to allow us entry into the Garibaldi House. In Italy, Teresa and Giuliano Vitali accompanied us to Sardinia where we explored Garibaldi's home, museum, and the beaches of the Emerald Coast. During our trip to Puglia, we were adopted by Agata Laviola and Andrea Roberto and their beautiful family and friends who introduced us to the joys of the Pugliese cuisine, culture, and lifestyle. For the record, Agata, were definitely coming back. We are grateful to Marianna Randazzo and the staff at the Garibaldi-Meucci Museum on Staten Island, New York for hosting our talk and book signing, and to Susan Suddeth and the Library staff at the University of South Carolina for giving us unfettered access to the extensive Campanella Collection of Garibaldi books and memorabilia.

The Garibaldi biographers Lucy Riall, Dennis Mack Smith, Alfonso Scirocco, Jasper Ridley, Christopher Hibbert, Giuseppe Abba, Peter de Polnay, Andrea Viotti, Theodore Dwight, and Giuseppe Garibaldi himself inspired us to go deep into our subject. University of South Carolina Professor and author Don Doyle was particularly generous with his time explaining Garibaldi's influences on the American Civil War.

To all writers whose works we have read and hope to read, we extend our appreciation for your talent, generosity and inspiration.

ABOUT THE AUTHORS

John and Nancy remain out in the world looking for adventures.

Visit their website: ThePetralias.com for new stories, favorite books, photos of their travels and more about Garibaldi. Connect with them on Facebook at "Not in a Tuscan Villa" or "John and Nancy Petralia / Authors." Most important, if you enjoyed the book, leave a review on Amazon.